PAGODA
BUSINESS BIBLE

Basic

PAGODA
BUSINESS
BIBLE Basic

Copyright © 2024 by PAGODA SCS

All rights reserved. No part of this publication may be reproduced, stored in a retrieval system, or transmitted, in any form, or by any means, electronic, mechanical, photocopying, recording or otherwise, without the prior written permission of the copyright holder and the publisher.

Published by PAGODA Books

PAGODA Books is the professional language publishing company of the PAGODA Education Group.
19F, PAGODA Tower, 419, Gangnam-daero,
Seocho-gu, Seoul, 06614, Rep. of KOREA
www.pagodabook.com

First published 2024
First impression 2024
Printed in the Republic of Korea

ISBN 978-89-6281-918-2 (13730)

Publisher | Kyung-Sil Park
Writer | PAGODA Language Education Center

A defective book may be exchanged at the store where you purchased it.

PAGODA

Basic
● MEETING | WRITING | PRESENTATION ●

This is
BUSINESS ENGLISH

BUSINESS BIBLE

PAGODA Books

목차

MEETING 7

First Meeting
1 Thank you for being here today. — 008

Meeting a New Coworker
2 It's your first day here, right? — 014

Scheduling a Meeting
3 Could we schedule a meeting sometime this week? — 020

Rescheduling
4 Could we move the meeting to a different time? — 026

Preparing a Venue for a Meeting
5 I'll reserve Conference Room 12. — 032

Inviting Attendees
6 Who will be attending the meeting? — 038

Suggesting Ideas
7 Does anyone have any suggestions? — 044

Disagreeing
8 I don't think that's a good idea. — 050

Deadlines and Schedules
9 When is the deadline for the sales report? — 056

Progress Report
10 Why don't you give us an update on the progress? — 062

Zoom/WebEX Meeting Expressions
11 Can everyone hear me okay? — 068

Zoom/WebEX Troubleshooting
12 My screen froze. — 074

Basic

WRITING 81

1	Starting an E-mail	082
2	Making Requests	090
3	Scheduling a Meeting	098
4	Agreeing to a Request for a Meeting	106
5	Rescheduling a Meeting	114
6	Congratulating Someone	122
7	Giving Instructions	130
8	Out-of-Office Message	138
9	Making Announcements	146
10	Sharing Good News	154
11	Writing Invitations	162
12	Holiday Greetings	170

PRESENTATION 179

1	Starting a Presentation	180
2	Stating the Topic and Main Points	188
3	Entertaining the Audience	196
4	Using Transitions	204
5	Giving Supporting Evidence and Examples	212
6	Emphasizing Key Points	220
7	Using Visuals 1	228
8	Using Visuals 2	236
9	Expressing Opinions and Recommendations	244
10	Summarizing Key Points	252
11	Closing	260
12	Answering Questions	268

PAGODA BUSINESS BIBLE

Basic

MEETING

1 First Meeting
Thank you for being here today.

Learning Objectives

- Learners can greet people at a meeting.
- Learners can thank people for attending a meeting.
- Learners can start a meeting.

Warm Up

Work with a partner or in a group. Discuss the following questions.

1. Why do people have meetings?
2. How often do you attend meetings?
3. What was the purpose of the last meeting that you attended?

Dialogue

Practice the dialogue with a partner.

A: Excuse me. Is this Conference Room 102?

B: Yes, it is. You must be from ABC Corp.

A: That's right. I'm Mary Ronan.

B: Pleasure to meet you, Mary. I'm Roger Peters by the way. **Thank you for being here today.**

A: **It's a pleasure to be here.** I've heard so many wonderful things about your products.

B: **I appreciate your interest in our products.**

A: Well, I'm here to learn more about them.

B: Of course. I think everyone is here now. **Should we start the meeting?**

A: 실례합니다. 여기가 102호 회의실인가요?
B: 네, 맞습니다. ABC 사에서 오셨죠?
A: 맞습니다. 전 Mary Ronan입니다.
B: 만나서 반갑습니다, Mary. 참, 저는 Roger Peters입니다. **오늘 여기 와 주셔서 감사합니다.**
A: **이 자리에 오게 되어 영광입니다.** 이쪽 제품에 대해 좋은 얘기를 많이 들었습니다.
B: **저희 제품에 관심을 가져주셔서 감사합니다.**
A: 당신의 제품에 대해서 더 알아보려 여기에 왔습니다.
B: 물론이죠. 이제 다들 모인 것 같네요. **회의를 시작할까요?**

✓ Comprehension Check

Answer the questions.

1. Which company does Mary Ronan work for?
2. Where are Mary and Roger talking?

 Vocabulary

Match the words or expressions with the correct definitions.

1. conference room _____   a. 그나저나
2. pleasure _____   b. 관심
3. by the way _____   c. 회의실
4. appreciate _____   d. ~에 감사해 하다
5. interest _____   e. 기쁨, 즐거움

⊕ Bonus Resources

get the ball rolling 일을 시작하다

A: Should we get started? 그럼 시작해 볼까요?
B: Sure! Let's **get the ball rolling**. 그럼요! 시작합시다.

get the ball rolling을 직역하면 '공이 굴러가도록 하다'라는 뜻이다. 즉, 업무가 순조롭게 진행되는 것을 부드럽게 굴러가는 공에 빗대어 생긴 숙어다.

Grammar Points

Read the following and practice making sentences.

1. Thank you for + ~ing

> Thank you for + ~ing는 '~해 주셔서 감사합니다'라는 뜻이다. Thank you 뒤에 'for'을 쓴다는 것에 유의하자.
>
> 📖 *Thank you for helping me.* 저를 도와주셔서 감사합니다.

a) Thank you for _____. 와주셔서 감사합니다.

b) Thank you for _____. 전화 주셔서 감사합니다.

c) Thank you for _____. 이해해 주셔서 감사합니다.

2. It's a pleasure to ~

> 'It'은 특별한 의미가 없지만 문장 구조상 필요한 주어 자리를 차지하는 역할을 한다. It's a pleasure to ~는 '~하는 것이 기쁨이다' 즉, '~하여 기쁘다'라는 의미로 처음 만났을 때 나누는 인사에 자주 쓰인다.
>
> 📖 *It's a pleasure to meet you.* 만나서 반가워요.

a) It's a pleasure to _____ with you. 당신과 함께 일하게 되어 기쁩니다.

b) It's a pleasure to _____ from you. 당신으로부터 소식을 듣게 되어 기쁩니다.

c) It's a pleasure to _____ our guest speaker. 저희 초청 연사를 소개하게 되어 기쁩니다.

✏ Write

Make your own dialogue using the expressions from Grammar Points.

A: _____

B: _____

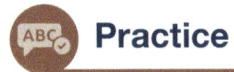 **Practice**

Shadowing

Listen and repeat.

1. **Thank you for** working with us.
   Thank you for coming.

2. **It's a pleasure to** attend the meeting.
   It's a pleasure to join you.

3. **I appreciate** your interest in the new model.
   I appreciate the advice.

4. **Should we** watch the video now?
   Should we have a snack?

5. Let's **get the ball rolling** with a team meeting.

Making Sentences

Practice making sentences. Use the words in the parentheses or use your own. Then, read your sentences to your partner or group. After sharing your sentences, practice saying someone else's sentences.

1. Thank you for _____. (be nice, understand, help)

2. It's a pleasure to _____. (meet, see, work)

3. I appreciate _____. (help, gift)

4. Should we _____? (go, try, plan)

Roleplay

Roleplay the following scenarios with a partner. Practice and change roles.

Scenario 1

Two sales managers from different companies meet for the first time.

Person 1: thank Person 2 for coming

Person 2: talk about Person 1's company's products or services / start the meeting

Scenario 2

Two people meet at a networking event.

Person 1: thank Person 2 for inviting you

Person 2: thank Person 1 for coming / suggest sitting down to talk

Homework

Write a short dialogue for your next meeting.

_____

_____

_____

Warm Up Sample Answers
1. People have meetings (to share ideas / to sell a product / to solve problems).
2. I attend meetings (once a month / every day).
3. The purpose of my last meeting was to brainstorm ideas.

Comprehension Check Answers
1. Mary Ronan works for ABC Corp.
2. They are talking in Conference Room 102.

Vocabulary Answers
1. c, 2. e, 3. a, 4. d, 5. b

Grammar Points Answers
1. a) coming b) calling c) understanding
2. a) work b) hear c) introduce

Write Sample Answer
A: Thank you for coming to my birthday party!
B: It's a pleasure to be here!

Making Sentences Sample Answers
1. Thank you for (being nice / understanding / helping).
2. It's a pleasure to (meet you / see you again / work with you).
3. I appreciate (your help / this gift).
4. Should we (go / try it / plan a party)?

Roleplay Sample Answer
Scenario 1
Person 1: Thank you for coming.
Person 2: It's a pleasure to meet you. We really appreciate your services. Should we start the meeting?

Homework Sample Answer
Person 1: Thank you for being here today. My name is Ronald Elderberry, senior manager. I appreciate your interest in our products. We are very excited to show you our new software.
Person 2: I'm Jasmine. It's a pleasure to be here. I'm very excited about your new AI imaging software.
Person 1: That's wonderful to hear. Should we start the meeting?
Person 2: Sure! Let's get the ball rolling.

Meeting Tip

How to Have Great Business Meetings
훌륭한 비즈니스 회의를 진행하는 방법

① **Decide on the goal for the meeting.** 회의의 목적을 정한다.
You should be able to say the purpose of the meeting in one short sentence before moving to the next step.
다음 단계로 넘어가기 전에 회의의 목적을 한 문장으로 짧게 말할 수 있어야 한다.

② **Invite only people who are necessary.** 필수적인 사람들만 초대한다.
Try to have fewer than 10 people. This will make the meeting easier to handle.
10명 미만으로 초대한다. 그래야 회의를 진행하기가 더 쉬워진다.

③ **Find a place to meet.** 만날 장소를 찾는다.
Consider the size and purpose of your meeting when choosing where to meet.
만날 장소를 선택할 때 회의의 규모와 목적을 고려한다.

④ **Prepare for the meeting.** 회의를 준비한다.
Prepare a plan that includes all the things needed to achieve your goal. Also, pick a person to write down the minutes.
목표를 달성하는 데 필요한 모든 사항이 포함된 계획을 준비한다. 또한, 회의록을 작성할 사람을 한 명 정한다.

⑤ **Plan for online meetings.** 온라인 회의를 계획한다.
Choose a person to help with technical issues, such as internet connectivity. Also, you should summarize the points often so that everyone follows the meeting.
인터넷 연결과 같은 기술적 문제를 해결할 사람 한 명을 선택한다. 또한, 모든 사람들이 회의를 따라오도록 요점을 자주 요약한다.

2 Meeting a New Coworker

It's your first day here, right?

 ### Learning Objectives

- Learners can welcome a new coworker.
- Learners can compliment a coworker.
- Learners can express excitement about joining a team or a company.

 ### Warm Up

Work with a partner or in a group. Discuss the following questions.

1. Have you ever welcomed a new coworker?
2. How did you feel on your first day at work?
3. What team or division are you part of?

 ### Dialogue

Practice the dialogue with a partner.

> A: **It's your first day here, right?** I'm Ken Waters.
>
> B: Hi! I'm Cindy Landon. It's a pleasure to meet you.
>
> A: **I've heard great things about you.**
>
> B: You have? Thank you.
>
> A: **It's great to have you on our team.**
>
> B: I'm so glad to be here. Will I be working on the Wilson Project?
>
> A: Yes, we'll be working on it together. **Let me fill you in on the current situation.**
>
> B: That would be great.

A: 오늘이 여기 첫 출근일이죠, 그렇죠? 저는 Ken Waters입니다.
B: 안녕하세요! 전 Cindy Landon입니다. 만나게 되어 기쁩니다.
A: 당신에 대해 좋은 이야기 많이 들었습니다.
B: 그러셨어요? 고맙습니다.
A: 우리 팀에 들어오시게 되어 기쁩니다.
B: 여기 오게 되어 정말 좋습니다. Wilson Project에 관한 일을 하게 되나요?
A: 네, 그 일을 함께 하게 될 겁니다. **현재 상황에 대해 알려드리죠.**
B: 그러면 너무 좋죠.

Comprehension Check

Answer the questions.

1. Whose first day is it?
2. What project will they be working on?

Vocabulary

Match the words or expressions with the correct definitions.

1. glad _____
2. work on _____
3. fill ~ in _____
4. current _____
5. situation _____

a. 기쁜, 좋은
b. 채워넣다
c. 상황
d. 현재의
e. ~에 관한 일을 하다

⊕ Bonus Resources

look forward to ~을 기대하다

A: It's great to have you join the project. 프로젝트에 합류하시게 되어 기쁩니다.
B: I **look forward to** working with everyone on the team.
팀원 모두와 함께 일하는 게 기대됩니다.

여기서 look은 '보다'이고 forward는 '앞으로'를 뜻한다. 이 두 단어를 합치면 '앞으로 보다'로 직역되는데, '기대하다'라는 의미다.

Grammar Points

Read the following and practice making sentences.

1. It's great to ~

> It's great to ~는 '~하게 되어 기쁘다, 좋다'라는 뜻으로, 뒤에 동사원형을 붙인다.
>
> *It's great to meet you finally.* 드디어 만나게 되어서 기쁩니다.

a) It's great to _____ in Korea. 한국에 오게 되어 기쁩니다.

b) It's great to _____ you. 뵙게 되어 기쁩니다.

c) It's great to _____ everyone here. 모두 여기에 모실 수 있어 기쁩니다.

2. Let me ~

> Let me ~ 뒤에 내가 하고자 하는 액션을 동사원형으로 붙이면 된다. 허락을 받는 게 아니라 내가 무엇을 하겠다는 선언이다.
>
> *Let me think.* 생각 좀 해 볼게요.

a) Let me _____ this first. 이거 먼저 끝낼게요.

b) Let me _____ Joe. Joe한테 전화할게요.

c) Let me _____ myself. 제 소개를 할게요.

Write

Make your own dialogue using the expressions from Grammar Points.

A: _____

B: _____

 **Practice**

Shadowing

Listen and repeat.

1. **It's your** first time in Korea, **right**?
   It's your second visit, **right**?

2. **I've heard great things about** the team.
   I've heard great things about your company.

3. **It's great to** see everyone again.
   It's great to be here.

4. **Let me** tell my boss that you're here.
   Let me see if he is in.

5. I **look forward to** the meeting.

Making Sentences

Practice making sentences. Use the words in the parentheses or use your own. Then, read your sentences to your partner or group. After sharing your sentences, practice saying someone else's sentences.

1. It's your _____, right? (time, visit)

2. I've heard great things about _____. (project, city, product)

3. It's great to _____. (see, talk, be)

4. Let me _____. (unpack, call, talk)

 ## Roleplay

Roleplay the following scenarios with a partner. Practice and change roles.

Scenario 1

A new employee meets his supervisor for the first time.
Person 1: welcome Person 2 to the team
Person 2: thank Person 1 / say it's great to be on the team

Scenario 2

Two new employees meet for the first time.
Person 1: ask if its Person 2's first day
Person 2: say yes and ask Person 1 the same question / ask if Person 1 has met the boss

 ## Homework

Write a short dialogue of two people meeting for the first time.

_____

_____

_____

Warm Up Sample Answers
1. (Yes, I have / No, I've never) welcomed a new coworker before.
2. I felt (excited/nervous/uncertain).
3. I'm part of (the overseas sales team / the accounting division / the purchasing team).

Comprehension Check Answers
1. It's Cindy Landon's first day.
2. They will be working on the Wilson Project.

Vocabulary Answers
1. a, 2. e, 3. b, 4. d, 5. c

Grammar Points Answers
1. a) be b) see c) have
2. a) finish b) call/phone c) introduce

Write Sample Answer
A: It's great to be finally here. Where will I be working?
B: Let me show you to your desk.

Making Sentences Sample Answers
1. It's your (third time here / first visit to Korea), right?
2. I've heard great things about (the project / the city / the product).
3. It's great to (see you / talk to you / be in the U.S.).
4. Let me (unpack first / call him / talk to her).

Roleplay Sample Answer
Scenario 1
Person 1: Hi, Linda. I'm John. It's your first day on the team, right? Welcome!
Person 2: Hi, John. Thanks. It's great to be on the team.

Homework Sample Answer
Person 1: You're Alan? It's your first day here, right?
Person 2: Ah, yes.
Person 1: I'm Karen. I've heard great things about you. It's great to have you on the team.
Person 2: I look forward to working with everyone.
Person 1: Let me fill you in on the current situation.

Meeting Tip

How to Enhance Your Nonverbal Skills
비언어적 의사소통 기술을 향상시키는 방법

①

Use eye contact. 눈맞춤을 한다.

Try to use good eye contact. Of course, you should look away occasionally.
적절하게 시선을 유지하도록 노력한다. 물론 가끔 눈길을 돌리는 것이 좋다.

②

Look expectant. 기대가 찬 표정을 한다.

Maintain an expectant look on your face while the other person is talking.
다른 사람이 말할 때 기대에 찬 표정을 유지한다.

③

Make a good impression. 좋은 인상을 준다.

Maintain a tidy appearance at all times. Also, having a good posture shows confidence.
늘 깔끔한 모습을 유지한다. 그리고 좋은 자세는 자신감을 보여준다.

④

Watch for nonverbal signals. 비언어적 표현을 잘 살핀다.

People reveal their thoughts through their expressions, gestures, and posture.
사람들은 얼굴 표정과 몸짓, 자세로 자신들의 생각을 들어낸다.

⑤

Be mindful of touching. 접촉에 주의한다.

In business, shaking hands firmly is considered good manners. However, other types of touching may not be appropriate.
비즈니스에서 굳게 악수하는 것은 좋은 매너로 간주된다. 그러나 다른 방식으로의 접촉은 적절하지 않을 수 있다.

Scheduling a Meeting

3 Could we schedule a meeting sometime this week?

Learning Objectives

- Learners can suggest a meeting date.
- Learners can ask when the best time to meet is.
- Learners can agree on a specific date to meet.

Warm Up

Work with a partner or in a group. Discuss the following questions.

1. Who usually decides when to have meetings at work?
2. Who usually leads the meetings?
3. Where do you usually have your meetings?

Dialogue

Practice the dialogue with a partner.

> A: We need to discuss the new project in Busan. **Could we schedule a meeting sometime this week?**
>
> B: Sure. This week sounds good. **When should we meet?**
>
> A: How about Wednesday?
>
> B: Oh, you know what? **I have another meeting that day.**
>
> A: Are you free on Thursday?
>
> B: Yes, I am. **How long do you think the meeting will take?**
>
> A: It should take a few hours. Should we have the meeting in my office?
>
> B: All right. I'll see you on Thursday.

A: 부산에서 신규 프로젝트에 대해 논의해야 합니다. **이번 주 언제 한번 회의 날짜를 잡을 수 있을까요?**
B: 그러죠. 이번 주 좋습니다. **언제 만날까요?**
A: 수요일 어떠세요?
B: 아, 그게요. **그날 다른 회의가 있습니다.**
A: 목요일은 시간 되세요?
B: 네, 됩니다. **회의가 얼마나 걸릴 것 같습니까?**
A: 몇 시간 걸릴 겁니다. 제 사무실에서 회의할까요?
B: 알겠습니다. 목요일에 뵐게요.

Comprehension Check

Answer the questions.

1. What day is the meeting on?
2. What will the two people be discussing?

Vocabulary

Match the words or expressions with the correct definitions.

1. schedule _____
2. sounds good _____
3. how about _____
4. free on _____
5. take _____

a. 괜찮다
b. (일정을) 잡다
c. ~에 시간 되는
d. 걸리다
e. ~ 어때요?

⊕ Bonus Resources

make it (on) 시간이 되다, 갈 수 있다

A: I can't **make it on** Monday. 월요일은 시간이 안 됩니다.
B: Me, neither. I have another meeting in the morning.
   저도요. 그날 아침 다른 회의가 있어요.

make를 직역하면 '만들다'가 되지만, 여기서는 '가다', '이르다'라는 의미가 되므로 어떤 곳에 갈 수 있다는 뜻이고 it은 해당 회의나 행사, 약속 등을 의미한다.

 **Grammar Points**

Read the following and practice making sentences.

1. Could we ~?

> Could we ~?는 '우리 ~해도 될까요?'라고 물을 때 쓰이며, 뒤에 동사원형을 붙인다.
>
> Ex *Could we go to lunch?* 우리 점심 식사 하러 가도 될까요?

    a) Could we _____ soon? 우리 곧 만날 수 있을까요?
    b) Could we _____ later? 나중에 얘기할 수 있을까요?
    c) Could we _____ a break? 휴식 시간을 가질 수 있을까요?

2. When should we ~?

> When should we ~?는 '언제 ~을 할 수 있나?'라고 물을 때 유용하게 쓸 수 있는 패턴으로, 뒤에 하고자 하는 행동을 동사원형으로 붙이면 된다.
>
> Ex *When should we start?* 언제 시작할까요?

    a) When should we _____ them? 언제 그들에게 말할까요?
    b) When should we _____ to New York? 언제 뉴욕으로 갈까요?
    c) When should we _____ lunch? 언제 점심 먹을까요?

✏ Write

Make your own dialogue using the expressions from Grammar Points.

A: _____

B: _____

 **Practice**

Shadowing

Listen and repeat.

1. **Could we** discuss the details now?
   Could we go now?

2. **When should we** tell the director?
   When should we send the e-mail?

3. **I have another meeting** in the afternoon.
   I have another meeting at 9 A.M.

4. **How long do you think** that will take?
   How long do you think the talk will last?

5. I can **make it on** Tuesday.

Making Sentences

Practice making sentences. Use the words in the parentheses or use your own. Then, read your sentences to your partner or group. After sharing your sentences, practice saying someone else's sentences.

1. Could we schedule a meeting for _____? (afternoon, today, tomorrow)

2. When should we _____? (respond, get together, finish)

3. I have another meeting _____. (scheduled, client, afternoon)

4. How long do you think _____? (meeting, presentation)

 **Roleplay**

Roleplay the following scenarios with a partner. Practice and change roles.

Scenario 1

Two people are trying to arrange a meeting.

Person 1: ask Person 2 to meet tomorrow morning

Person 2: tell Person 1 that you have another meeting then / suggest another date

Scenario 2

Two people are talking about a meeting on Monday.

Person 1: ask if Person 2 can make the meeting on Monday

Person 2: say it's possible and ask how long the meeting will take

 **Homework**

Write a short dialogue of two people attempting to schedule a meeting.

___

___

___

Warm Up Sample Answers
1. Usually (my boss / a fellow team member) decides when to have meetings.
2. Usually (my boss / the department manager) leads the meetings.
3. I usually have meetings (at my company / outside the company / at a client's office).

Comprehension Check Answers
1. The meeting is on Thursday.
2. They will be discussing the new project in Busan.

Vocabulary Answers
1. b, 2. a, 3. e, 4. c, 5. d

Grammar Points Answers
1. a) meet b) talk c) take
2. a) tell b) go c) have/eat

Write Sample Answer
A: When should we meet?
B: Could we meet this Friday?

Making Sentences Sample Answers
1. Could we schedule a meeting for (this afternoon / today / tomorrow)?
2. When should we (respond to the e-mail / get together / finish the meeting)?
3. I have another meeting (scheduled / with a client / in the afternoon).
4. How long do you think (the meeting will take / the presentation will last)?

Roleplay Sample Answer
Scenario 1
Person 1: Could we schedule a meeting for tomorrow morning?
Person 2: I'm sorry, but I have another meeting tomorrow morning. How about Wednesday?

Homework Sample Answer
Person 1: When should we meet?
Person 2: Could we schedule a meeting sometime this week? What about Thursday?
Person 1: I have another meeting that day.
Person 2: How long do you think the meeting will take?
Person 1: It will take a while. I can make it on Friday though.
Person 2: Friday? Okay. That sounds good.

Meeting Tip

Deciding on the Best Place and Time for a Meeting
회의하기에 가장 좋은 장소와 시간 정하기

① Design a seating plan. 좌석 배치안을 설계한다.

Think about the size of the meeting room. Then consider the seating arrangement of the attendees.
회의실의 크기를 생각해 본다. 그다음 참석자들의 좌석 배치를 고려한다.

② Atmosphere is important. 분위기는 중요하다.

If you can, adjust the temperature and lighting beforehand. Also, have some refreshments ready.
가능하다면 온도와 조명을 미리 조정한다. 그리고 다과도 준비한다.

③ Schedule meetings in the morning. 아침 시간에 회의를 잡는다.

Conduct meetings in the morning if possible. People tend to be more alert and able to focus better.
되도록이면 아침에 회의를 진행한다. 사람들은 정신이 더 맑고 집중을 더 잘하기 마련이다.

④ Take advantage of virtual meetings. 화상 회의를 이용한다.

If the attendees are in different locations, virtual meetings may be the best way to connect.
참석자들이 여러 곳에 있다면, 화상 회의가 서로 연결하기에 가장 좋은 방법일 수 있다.

⑤ Avoid Friday afternoon meetings. 금요일 오후 회의는 피한다.

On Friday afternoons, most people are not thinking about work. Their minds are on the weekend ahead.
금요일 오후에는 대부분의 사람들이 일에 대해 생각하고 있지 않다. 그들의 정신은 주말에 집중되어 있다.

4 Rescheduling
Could we move the meeting to a different time?

 Learning Objectives

- Learners can suggest rescheduling a meeting.
- Learners can suggest alternate dates to meet.
- Learners can agree on a new date to meet.

 Warm Up

Work with a partner or in a group. Discuss the following questions.

1. Have you ever had to change a meeting date?
2. Do you keep a planner?
3. What are some reasons people might change a meeting date?

 Dialogue

Practice the dialogue with a partner.

> A: Hi, Peter.
>
> B: Hello, Mark. What's up?
>
> A: It's about our meeting. Something came up. **Could we move the meeting to a different time?**
>
> B: Sure. **I'm available on Friday morning.** Does that work for you?
>
> A: Actually, I will be on a business trip. I won't be back until the following week.
>
> B: Okay, what's a good date for you?
>
> A: Let's see. **How about Thursday afternoon?** Say, 3 P.M.?
>
> B: **Thursday sounds good to me.** See you at 3.

A: 안녕하세요, Peter.
B: 안녕하세요, Mark. 무슨 일이세요?
A: 우리 회의에 대해서인데요. 다른 일이 생겨서요. **회의를 다른 시간으로 바꿔도 될까요?**
B: 그러죠. **금요일 아침에 시간이 됩니다.** 가능하세요?
A: 실은 출장 중일 겁니다. 그다음 주까지 돌아오지 않을 겁니다.
B: 그럼, 어느 날짜가 좋으시겠어요?
A: 보자. **목요일 오후 어떠세요?** 뭐, 오후 3시?
B: **목요일 좋습니다.** 3시에 봐요.

Comprehension Check

Answer the questions.

1. What day does Peter suggest moving the meeting to?
2. Why can't Mark meet on Friday?

Vocabulary

Match the words or expressions with the correct definitions.

1. come up _____
2. work for (someone) _____
3. on a business trip _____
4. the following week _____
5. to me _____

a. 출장 중
b. 그다음 주, 차주
c. (일이) 생기다
d. 저에게는
e. (~에게는) 가능하다

⊕ Bonus Resources

get back to (someone)
(답변을 주려고) 나중에 다시 연락하다

A: How about Thursday afternoon? 목요일 오후 어떠세요?
B: I'll **get back to you**. I might have another meeting then.
다시 연락드릴게요. 그때 다른 회의가 있을 수 있어서요.

get back이라고 하면 '다시 돌아오다'라는 뜻이 먼저 떠오르기 마련인데, 답변을 줘야하는 상황에서 get back to someone은 누군가에게 '다시 연락하다'라는 의미가 된다.

Grammar Points

Read the following and practice making sentences.

1. I'm available ~

> available은 '여유 있는', '시간이 되는'을 뜻하므로, I'm available ~은 '해당 시간이나 날짜에 만날 여유나 시간이 있다'라는 의미가 있으며, 흔히 뒤에 전치사가 붙는다.
>
> 📖 *I'm available next week.* 다음 주에 시간이 됩니다.

a) I'm available on _____. 수요일에 시간이 됩니다.

b) I'm available at _____. 오전 11시에 시간이 됩니다.

c) I'm available in the _____. 오후에 시간이 됩니다.

2. How about ~?

> How about ~?은 표현 그대로 '~은 어때요?'를 뜻하는 아주 유용한 패턴으로, 뒤에 제안하는 것이나 날짜 등을 붙이면 된다.
>
> 📖 *How about January?* 1월 어떠세요?

a) How about _____ next week? 다음 주 중으로 어떠세요?

b) How about _____? 오늘 어떠세요?

c) How about _____ office? 그쪽 사무실 어떠세요?

✏️ Write

Make your own dialogue using the expressions from Grammar Points.

A: _____

B: _____

 **Practice**

Shadowing

Listen and repeat.

1. **Could we move the meeting to** tomorrow?
   Could we move the meeting to next week?

2. **I'm available** now.
   I'm available in the mornings.

3. **How about** this evening?
   How about next month?

4. Monday **sounds good to me**.
   Next week **sounds good to me**.

5. I'll **get back to you** tomorrow.

Making Sentences

Practice making sentences. Use the words in the parentheses or use your own. Then, read your sentences to your partner or group. After sharing your sentences, practice saying someone else's sentences.

1. Could we move the meeting to _____? (different, another)

2. I'm available _____. (month, after, anytime)

3. How about _____? (now, tonight)

4. _____ sounds good to me. (that, year, weekend)

Roleplay

Roleplay the following scenarios with a partner. Practice and change roles.

Scenario 1

Two people are trying to reschedule a meeting.
Person 1: ask Person 2 to meet on a different date
Person 2: tell Person 1 you're available next month

Scenario 2

Two people are trying to agree on a new meeting date.
Person 1: ask if Person 2 is available on Thursday
Person 2: say it's your day off / suggest meeting on Friday

Homework

Write a short dialogue of two people trying to reschedule a meeting.

Warm Up Sample Answers
1. Yes, I have had to change a meeting date (before / several times). / No, I never have.
2. (Yes, I do / No, I don't) keep a planner.
3. People may change a meeting date due to (a scheduling conflict / a personal matter / an unexpected problem).

Comprehension Check Answers
1. He suggests moving the meeting to Friday.
2. He will be on a business trip.

Vocabulary Answers
1. c, 2. e, 3. a, 4. b, 5. d

Grammar Points Answers
1. a) Wednesday b) 11 A.M. c) afternoon
2. a) sometime b) today c) your

Write Sample Answer
A: I'm available anytime next week.
B: How about Monday, then?

Making Sentences Sample Answers
1. Could we move the meeting to (a different day / another time)?
2. I'm available (this month / after 5 P.M. / anytime).
3. How about (now / tonight)?
4. (That / This year / Next weekend) sounds good to me.

Roleplay Sample Answer
Scenario 1
Person 1: Could we move the meeting to a different date?
Person 2: Sure. I'm available next month. What's a good day for you?

Homework Sample Answer
Person 1: Could we move the meeting to a different time?
Person 2: Sure. I'm available on Friday morning.
Person 1: How about Thursday afternoon?
Person 2: Thursday sounds good to me. What time do you want to meet?
Person 1: I'll get back to you on that.
Person 2: Okay. Give me a call.

> **Meeting Tip**

Etiquette Is Very Important in Business Settings
에티켓은 비즈니스 현장에서 매우 중요하다

① Pay attention to personal grooming. 개인적인 차림새에 신경쓴다.

Always be mindful of cleanliness. Comb or brush your hair and avoid strong perfumes and colognes.

늘 청결에 유의하자. 머리를 잘 빗고 향이 강한 향수는 피한다.

② Dress for success. 성공을 위한 옷을 입는다.

Dress in a simple manner, and avoid clothes that may be considered inappropriate for business.

깔끔한 옷차림을 하며 비즈니스상 적절하지 않다고 간주되는 옷은 피한다.

③ Be courteous and professional on the phone.
통화 중에 정중하고 전문적으로 행동한다.

People use the phone frequently during the workday. Speak clearly, and always remain professional on the phone.

사람들은 근무 시간 동안 전화를 자주 쓴다. 통화 중에 또렷하게 말을 하고 늘 프로답게 처신한다.

④ Keep your workspace clean and tidy. 작업 공간을 깨끗하고 깔끔하게 유지한다.

How your desk looks says a lot about you, so keep your workspace looking tidy at all times.

나의 책상의 상태는 나에 대해 많은 걸 보여주는 만큼, 나의 작업 공간을 항상 깔끔하게 유지한다.

⑤ Answer e-mails promptly. 이메일에 즉시 답변한다.

Don't wait too long to answer e-mails. Many coworkers, customers, or vendors may be awaiting your answer.

이메일에 답변을 너무 오래 미루지 말자. 다수의 동료와 고객, 납품업체들이 나의 답변을 기다리고 있을 수 있다.

5 Preparing a Venue for a Meeting
I'll reserve Conference Room 12.

 Learning Objectives

- Learners can talk about choosing the venue for a meeting.
- Learners can volunteer to reserve a room for a meeting.
- Learners can discuss how to operate an equipment in a room.

 Warm Up

Work with a partner or in a group. Discuss the following questions.

1. Where do you usually have your internal meetings?
2. How many people usually attend the meetings?
3. How involved are you in preparing a room for a meeting?

 Dialogue

Practice the dialogue with a partner.

> A: Are we all set for the meeting on Monday?
> B: Oh, we need to reserve a room.
> A: I'll do it. **I'll reserve Conference Room 12.**
> B: **We need a room that can accommodate 10 people.** Is the room big enough?
> A: Yes, but I think there are only 8 chairs. **I think we can borrow more chairs from another room.**
> B: That's good. **Do you know how to use the overhead projector?**
> A: Yes, I do. I'll set it up before the meeting.
> B: Great.

A: 월요일 회의 준비가 다 됐나요?
B: 아, 회의실을 예약해야 합니다.
A: 제가 하죠. **12번 회의실 예약할게요.**
B: **10명을 수용할 수 있는 방이 필요합니다.** 그 방 크기 충분한가요?
A: 네, 그런데 의자가 8개밖에 없는 것 같아요. **다른 방에서 더 많은 의자를 빌리면 될 것 같습니다.**
B: 잘됐네요. **오버헤드 프로젝터 사용할 줄 아세요?**
A: 네, 알죠. 회의 시작 전에 세팅해 놓겠습니다.
B: 좋습니다.

✓ Comprehension Check

Answer the questions.

1. What room will the meeting be held in?
2. How many chairs are there in the room?

Vocabulary

Match the words or expressions with the correct definitions.

1. all set _____
2. reserve _____
3. accommodate _____
4. another _____
5. set ~ up _____

a. ~을 세팅하다, 준비하다
b. 수용하다
c. 예약하다
d. 다른, 또 하나의
e. 준비가 다 된

⊕ Bonus Resources

send out 발송하다

A: I'll reserve a conference room. 제가 회의실을 예약하겠습니다.
B: And I'll **send out** the agenda to everyone.
그럼 저는 의제를 모두에게 발송할게요.

send는 '보내다'로, send out은 '내보내다'가 되면서, 무언가를 '발송하다'라고 할 때 자주 쓰는 표현이다.

Grammar Points

Read the following and practice making sentences.

1. I think we can ~

> We can ~보다는 덜 확실한 가능성을 말하는 표현으로 I think we can ~은 '아마'라는 뉘앙스가 담긴 패턴이며 뒤에 동사원형이 붙는다.
>
> *I think we can ask the accountant.* 회계사에게 물어보면 될 것 같습니다.

a) I think we can _____ now. 지금 가도 될 것 같습니다.

b) I think we can _____ one. 하나 가져가도 될 것 같습니다.

c) I think we can _____ together. 함께 일하면 될 것 같습니다.

2. Do you know how to ~?

> Do you know how to ~?는 무언가를 하거나 사용할 줄 아느냐고 물을 때 유용한 패턴으로, 뒤에 동사원형을 붙이면 된다.
>
> *Do you know how to connect the cable?* 케이블 연결할 줄 아세요?

a) Do you know how to _____ Spanish? 스페인어 할 줄 아세요?

b) Do you know how to _____ the photo? 이 사진을 업로드할 줄 아세요?

c) Do you know how to _____ the Korean keyboard? 한국 키보드 쓸 줄 아세요?

✏ Write

Make your own dialogue using the expressions from Grammar Points.

A: _____

B: _____

Practice

Shadowing

Listen and repeat.

1. **I'll reserve** two rooms.
   I'll reserve a large room.
2. **We need a room** near the lobby.
   We need a room that has a long table.
3. **I think we can** call him now.
   I think we can take a short break.
4. **Do you know how to** use this?
   Do you know how to reserve a room?
5. I'll **send out** an e-mail tomorrow.

Making Sentences

Practice making sentences. Use the words in the parentheses or use your own. Then, read your sentences to your partner or group. After sharing your sentences, practice saying someone else's sentences.

1. I'll reserve _____. (second floor, small)
2. We need a room _____. (meeting, whiteboard, nearby)
3. I think we can _____. (discuss, ask, do)
4. Do you know how to _____? (set up, unlock, read)

Roleplay

Roleplay the following scenarios with a partner. Practice and change roles.

Scenario 1

Two people are talking about reserving a room.
Person 1: tell Person 2 that you need a large room
Person 2: tell Person 1 that you'll reserve Conference Room 1

Scenario 2

Two people are talking about preparing for a meeting.
Person 1: ask if Person 2 can reserve a room for the meeting
Person 2: say you will / ask if Person 1 knows how to connect the laptop and use the overhead projector

Homework

Write a short dialogue of two people talking about reserving a meeting room.

Warm Up Sample Answers
1. I usually have internal meetings (in my office / in a small conference room / in a large room).
2. Usually (only a few people / 3 or 4 people / a lot of people) attend the meetings.
3. (I'm / I'm not) very involved in preparing a room for a meeting.

Comprehension Check Answers
1. The meeting will be held in Conference Room 12.
2. There are 8 chairs.

Vocabulary Answers
1. e, 2. c, 3. b, 4. d, 5. a

Grammar Points Answers
1. a) go b) take c) work
2. a) speak b) upload c) use

Write Sample Answer
A: Do you know how to use this kiosk?
B: I think we can ask the clerk over there.

Making Sentences Sample Answers
1. I'll reserve (a conference room on the second floor / a small room).
2. We need a room (for the meeting / with a whiteboard / nearby).
3. I think we can (discuss it later / ask at the meeting / do that).
4. Do you know how to (set up an account / unlock the door / read this)?

Roleplay Sample Answer
Scenario 1
Person 1: We need a large room for the meeting.
Person 2: I'll reserve Conference Room 1.

Homework Sample Answer
Person 1: We need a room that can accommodate 10 people.
Person 2: I'll reserve Conference Room 12. That's big enough for 10 people. We will need more chairs, though.
Person 1: I think we can borrow more chairs from another room. Can you also send out the agenda?
Person 2: Sure. Do you know how to use the overhead projector?
Person 1: Actually, no. And I need to hook up my laptop.
Person 2: I can help you do that.

Meeting Tip

Choosing from Six Main Types of Meeting Room Configurations
6가지 주요 회의실 배치 유형 중 하나를 고르기

① Boardroom / Conference Style 이사회실 / 학회 배열

This is probably the most common setup, with a long table and chairs around it.

가장 흔한 배열로, 긴 테이블이 있고 여러 의자들이 긴 테이블을 둘러쌓는 구조다.

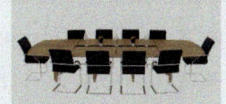

② Hollow square Style 공백 사각형 배열

Multiple tables are set up to form a square, with the leader / moderator inside the square.

여러 테이블로 정사각형을 이루고, 중간에 회의 진행자가 배치된다.

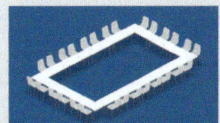

③ U-shape Style U형 배열

Tables are set up to form a U-shape. It's good for making presentations.

테이블들을 U자형으로 배치한다. 프레젠테이션에 유용하다.

④ Auditorium Style 강당 배열

This style is good for lectures, especially large groups.

특히 커다란 그룹을 위한 강의에 좋은 방식이다.

⑤ Classroom Style 교실 배열

Good for long lectures or talks, the room is set up like a regular classroom.

긴 강의나 회담에 좋은 방식으로, 방이 일반 교실처럼 세팅된다.

⑥ Banquet Style 연회 배열

As the name suggests, there are separate round tables, which is good for discussions.

이름이 말해주듯, 개별적인 원형 테이블들이 있어서 논의하기에 알맞다.

6 Inviting Attendees

Who will be attending the meeting?

Learning Objectives

- Learners can ask who will be attending a meeting.
- Learners can talk about contacting people for a meeting.
- Learners can express the importance of certain people attending a meeting.

Warm Up

Work with a partner or in a group. Discuss the following questions.

1. How often are you asked to attend meetings?
2. Do you ever have to miss a meeting?
3. Have you ever had to invite people to attend a meeting?

Dialogue

Practice the dialogue with a partner.

A: **Who will be attending the meeting?**

B: We've invited all the teams involved in the Patterson project.

A: What about the server team? **They have to come to the meeting.**

B: I did email them yesterday. **I haven't heard back from them yet.**

A: Well, again, it's important that they come to the meeting.

B: I agree. I'll call them after lunch.

A: Great. Oh, by the way, does the R&D team know the meeting is on July 2?

B: They should. **I'll contact them to confirm the meeting date.**

A: 누가 회의에 참석할 건가요?
B: Patterson 프로젝트와 관련된 모든 팀을 초대했습니다.
A: 서버팀은요? **그분들이 회의에 참석해야 하는데요.**
B: 어제 메일을 보내긴 했습니다. **아직 답변을 못 받았습니다.**
A: 뭐, 다시 말하지만, 그분들이 참석하는 것이 중요해요.
B: 동의합니다. 점심 후 전화해 볼게요.
A: 좋아요. 아, 참, R&D 팀이 회의를 7월 2일에 한다는 건 알고 있나요?
B: 그럴 겁니다. **그쪽에 연락해서 회의 날짜를 컨펌하겠습니다.**

Comprehension Check

Answer the questions.

1. What team has to come to the meeting?
2. Who will be contacted to confirm the meeting date?

Vocabulary

Match the words or expressions with the correct definitions.

1. involved in _____
2. hear back _____
3. important _____
4. agree _____
5. confirm _____

a. 중요한
b. 컨펌하다, 확인하다
c. 답변을 받다
d. ~와 관련된
e. 동의하다

⊕ Bonus Resources

follow up 확인 연락을 하다, 더 알아보다, 후속 조치를 취하다

A: I haven't heard from them yet. 아직 그 분들의 답변을 듣지 못했습니다.
B: Maybe you should **follow up** with them. 확인 연락 해봐야 할 것 같은데요.

'따라가다', '뒤를 잇다'라는 뜻을 가진 follow에 '계속하여', '유지하여'를 의미하는 up을 붙여서 '더 알아보다'가 되는 표현이다.

Grammar Points

Read the following and practice making sentences.

1. Who will be + ~ing ~?

> Who will be + ~ing ~?는 '무언가를 누가 할 것인가'를 묻는 표현으로 뒤에 해당 행위가 ~ing로 붙는다.
>
> *Who will be leading the meeting?* 누가 회의를 진행할 건가요?

a) Who will be _____ there? 누가 거기로 갈 건가요?
b) Who will be _____ the call? 누가 전화를 걸 건가요?
c) Who will be _____ to the event? 누가 행사에 올 건가요?

2. I'll contact them to ~

> them은 '그들', '그쪽'을 의미하며, I'll은 I will의 줄임말로, I will contact them to ~는 '그쪽으로 연락해서 ~을 하겠다'를 뜻한다.
>
> *I'll contact them to suggest it.* 그쪽에 연락해서 제안해 보겠습니다.

a) I'll contact them to _____ them the number. 그쪽에 연락해서 번호를 주겠습니다.
b) I'll contact them to _____ for the price. 그쪽에 연락해서 가격을 물어보겠습니다.
c) I'll contact them to _____ them know. 그쪽에 연락해서 알려주겠습니다.

✎ Write

Make your own dialogue using the expressions from Grammar Points.

A: _____

B: _____

 **Practice**

Shadowing

Listen and repeat.

1. **Who will be** com**ing** to the meeting?
   Who will be work**ing** on the project?

2. **They have to** ask us.
   They have to let us know.

3. **I haven't heard back from** the owner.
   I haven't heard back from the supplier.

4. **I'll contact them to** tell them about the problem.
   I'll contact them to ask for the proposal.

5. I'll **follow up** this afternoon.

Making Sentences

Practice making sentences. Use the words in the parentheses or use your own. Then, read your sentences to your partner or group. After sharing your sentences, practice saying someone else's sentences.

1. Who will be _____? (send, write)

2. They have to _____. (finish, do, sign)

3. I haven't heard back from _____. (boss, manufacturer)

4. I'll contact them to _____. (set up, rush, make)

 ## Roleplay

Roleplay the following scenarios with a partner. Practice and change roles.

Scenario 1

> **Two people are talking about some people attending a meeting.**
>
> **Person 1:** ask Person 2 who is coming to the meeting
>
> **Person 2:** tell Person 1 that the director is coming / you haven't heard back from the vice-president

Scenario 2

> **Two people are talking about a particular person attending a meeting.**
>
> **Person 1:** ask Person 2 if a certain person is coming to the meeting
>
> **Person 2:** tell Person 1 that you will contact that person

 ## Homework

Write a short dialogue of two people talking about who will be attending an upcoming meeting.

_____

_____

_____

Warm Up Sample Answers
1. I'm asked to attend meetings (once a week / several times a month / once a month).
2. Yes, sometimes I have to miss a meeting.
3. Yes, I have. / No, I haven't.

Comprehension Check Answers
1. The server team has to come to the meeting.
2. The R&D team will be contacted.

Vocabulary Answers
1. d, 2. c, 3. a, 4. e, 5. b

Grammar Points Answers
1. a) going b) making c) coming
2. a) give b) ask c) let

Write Sample Answer
A: Who will be making the presentation?
B: I'll contact them to ask about that.

Making Sentences Sample Answers
1. Who will be (sending out the notice / writing the report)?
2. They have to (finish on time / do the work / sign the contract).
3. I haven't heard back from (my boss / the manufacturer).
4. I'll contact them to (set up a meeting / rush the order / make the change).

Roleplay Sample Answer
Scenario 1
Person 1: Who will be coming to the meeting?
Person 2: The director is coming. But I haven't heard back from the vice-president yet.

Homework Sample Answer
Person 1: Who will be attending the meeting?
Person 2: Let's see. John, Mark, and Lynn have confirmed they will be attending.
Person 1: What about the suppliers? They have to come to the meeting.
Person 2: I haven't heard back from them yet. I will follow up today.
Person 1: Okay. They all know that the meeting has moved to this Friday, right?
Person 2: I'll contact them to confirm the meeting date.

Meeting Tip

Invite Only a Few People to Meetings
회의에는 적은 인원만 초대한다

① Decide on who should attend. 누가 참석할지 정한다.

Make a list and decide who really needs to attend the meeting and who doesn't. All attendees should participate in the discussion.

명단을 작성해서 회의에 누가 확실히 참석해야 하고 누가 안 와도 되는지 결정한다. 모든 참석자들은 논의에 참여하는 게 원칙이다.

② Keep reps to a minimum. 대표자를 최소한으로 유지한다.

Ask each team to send just one or two persons.

각 팀에게 한 명이나 두 명만 보내달라고 요청한다.

③ Make decisions quicker. 빠르게 결정한다.

If there are too many people, decisions take longer to make. With fewer people, reaching consensus will be easier.

사람이 너무 많으면 결정하는 데 시간이 더 오래 걸리기 마련이다. 사람이 적을수록 의견 일치가 더 수월해진다.

④ Share the minutes with non-attendees. 비참석자들에게 회의 내용을 공유한다.

After the meeting, send out the meeting minutes to non-attendees who may benefit from them.

회의 종료 후, 회의 내용을 알면 도움이 될 만한 비참석자들에게 회의록을 보낸다.

⑤ Exceptions exist. 예외는 있다.

Sometimes you have to make exceptions. For example, having a large number of attendees may be unavoidable for conferences.

때로는 예외를 둬야 할 때가 있다. 예를 들어, 콘퍼런스에서는 많은 참석자들의 참여가 불가피할 수 있다.

7 Suggesting Ideas

Does anyone have any suggestions?

Learning Objectives

- Learners can ask others if they have suggestions.
- Learners can make suggestions.
- Learners can react appropriately to suggestions.

Warm Up

Work with a partner or in a group. Discuss the following questions.

1. Do you enjoy making suggestions?
2. How often do you make suggestions during meetings?
3. Why are suggestions important during meetings?

Dialogue

Practice the dialogue with a partner.

A: All right, let's start with new marketing ideas. **Does anyone have any suggestions?**

B: **I was thinking we could create a social media campaign.**

A: Okay, Cindy. Social media campaign sounds good. What did you have in mind?

B: Maybe consumers can take photos of our stores or food and post them on social media.

A: Like on Instagram or blogs? **That's a great idea.**

B: And then we can choose the best photos and give out awards. We can do that at a nice ballroom somewhere.

A: **We should look into renting a venue.**

B: I'll look into it and come up with a list.

A: 자, 새로운 마케팅 아이디어로 시작합시다. **뭔가 제의할 만한 분 있나요?**
B: **SNS 캠페인을 시작하면 어떨까 생각했습니다.**
A: 그래요, Cindy. SNS 캠페인 좋지요. 뭐 생각한 거 있어요?
B: 소비자들이 저희 가게들이나 음식 사진을 찍어서 SNS에 포스팅할 수 있지 않을까 해요.
A: 인스타그램이나 블로그 같은 곳에요? **훌륭한 생각입니다.**
B: 그런 다음 가장 좋은 사진을 선정하고 상을 주는 겁니다. 어디 좋은 연회장에서 하면 되고요.
A: **빌릴 수 있는 장소를 알아봐야겠어요.**
B: 알아보고 명단을 만들어 보겠습니다.

Comprehension Check

Answer the questions.

1. What kind of campaign does Cindy suggest creating?
2. What kind of photos will consumers take?

Vocabulary

Match the words or expressions with the correct definitions.

1. start with _____
2. have in mind _____
3. give out _____
4. venue _____
5. come up with _____

a. ~을 생각해 내다
b. ~로 시작하다
c. ~을 생각하다
d. (행사, 회담 등의) 장소
e. ~을 나눠 주다

⊕ Bonus Resources

speak up 의견을 확실히 밝히다, 생각을 말하다

A: I was thinking we could hire a consultant.
　컨설턴트를 고용하면 어떨까 생각했습니다.
B: Does anyone have other suggestions? If you do, **speak up**.
　다른 제안이 있는 분 있나요? 있으면 확실히 말해 봐요.

speak up은 '너 크게 말하다'라는 뜻도 되지만 의견을 교환하는 상황에서는 자신의 '의견이나 생각을 주저 없이 밝히다'라는 의미가 된다.

Grammar Points

Read the following and practice making sentences.

1. Does anyone have ~?

> Does anyone have ~?는 함께 있는 사람들 중 누구든 의견이나 생각을 제시할 게 있는지 또는 질문이 있는지 물을 때 쓰는 표현이다.
>
> *Does anyone have any ideas?* 아이디어 가진 분 있나요?

a) Does anyone have any _____? 질문 있는 분 있나요?
b) Does anyone have _____ to offer? 뭐라도 제시할 분 있나요?
c) Does anyone have a _____? 제안 하실 분 있나요?

2. I was thinking we could ~

> I was thinking we could ~는 '할 수 있다'를 뜻하는 We could에 I was thinking을 앞에 붙여 의견을 정중하게 제시할 때 유용하다.
>
> *I was thinking we could find a new venue.* 새로운 장소를 찾으면 어떨까 생각했습니다.

a) I was thinking we could _____ the meeting early. 일찍 회의를 마무리하면 어떨까 생각했습니다.
b) I was thinking we could _____ some ideas. 아이디어를 브레인스토밍하면 어떨까 생각했습니다.
c) I was thinking we could _____ tomorrow. 내일 계속하면 어떨까 생각했습니다.

Write

Make your own dialogue using the expressions from Grammar Points.

A: _____

B: _____

 ## Practice

Shadowing

Listen and repeat.

1. **Does anyone have** a new suggestion?
   Does anyone have a different opinion?

2. **I was thinking we could** follow Jane's suggestion.
   I was thinking we could start the event early.

3. **That's** an interesting idea.
   That's a fantastic idea.

4. **We should look into** changing our logo.
   We should look into forming a partnership.

5. If you disagree, you need to **speak up.**

Making Sentences

Practice making sentences. Use the words in the parentheses or use your own. Then, read your sentences to your partner or group. After sharing your sentences, practice saying someone else's sentences.

1. Does anyone have _____? (something, comments)

2. I was thinking we could _____. (ask, go, start)

3. That's _____ idea. (good, nice, innovative)

4. We should look into _____. (visit, work)

Roleplay

Roleplay the following scenarios with a partner. Practice and change roles.

Scenario 1

Meeting attendees are talking about making some suggestions.

Person 1: ask if anyone has any suggestions

Person 2: suggest creating a new website

Scenario 2

Meeting attendees are talking about new suggestions.

Person 1: ask if Person 2 has any new suggestions

Person 2: tell Person 1 about a new product design idea

Homework

Write a short dialogue of two people talking about a suggestion during a meeting.

_____

_____

_____

Warm Up Sample Answers
1. (Yes, I enjoy / No, I don't enjoy) making suggestions.
2. I make (some / a lot of) suggestions during meetings.
3. Suggestions are important because (members can share ideas / new ideas can help solve problems).

Comprehension Check Answers
1. Cindy suggests creating a social media campaign.
2. Consumers will take photos of the stores or food.

Vocabulary Answers
1. b, 2. c, 3. e, 4. d, 5. a

Grammar Points Answers
1. a) questions b) something c) suggestion/proposal
2. a) end b) brainstorm c) continue

Write Sample Answer
A: Does anyone have an opinion?
B: I was thinking we could change the design.

Making Sentences Sample Answers
1. Does anyone have (something to add / any comments)?
2. I was thinking we could (ask them / go to Busan / start all over).
3. That's (a good / a nice / an innovative) idea.
4. We should look into (visiting the factory / working with a new accountant).

Roleplay Sample Answer
Scenario 1
Person 1: Does anyone have any suggestions?
Person 2: I was thinking we could create a new website.

Homework Sample Answer
Person 1: Does anyone have any suggestions? If you do, please speak up.
Person 2: I was thinking we could create a social media campaign.
Person 1: Okay.
Person 2: Maybe we can kick off with an event.
Person 1: That's a great idea. We should look into renting a venue.
Person 2: I have a venue in mind.

Meeting Tip

Five Stages of Effective Listening
효과적인 경청의 다섯 단계

① **Listening** 듣기

Listening begins with intentionally focusing on the speaker's message.
경청은 해당 화자의 발언에 고의로 집중하면서 시작된다.

② **Understanding** 이해하기

Then you decode what is being said by trying to understand the meaning of words and expressions.
그런 다음 단어와 표현들을 이해하려고 하면서 언급되고 있는 말을 해독한다.

③ **Remembering** 기억하기

In this stage, you add the message to your memory for future use.
이 단계에서는 미래에 사용하기 위해 메시지를 기억해 둔다.

④ **Evaluating** 평가하기

Here, you try and judge the value of the message by using your critical thinking skills.
여기서는 비판적 사고 기술을 사용해서 메시지의 가치를 판단하려고 한다.

⑤ **Reacting** 반응하기

You are now responding and giving your feedback to the message you heard.
이제는 들은 메시지에 반응을 하면서 피드백을 제시한다.

8 Disagreeing

I don't think that's a good idea.

 Learning Objectives

- Learners can disagree with a suggestion or opinion.
- Learners can explain the reason for disagreeing.
- Learners can say someone has made a good point.

 Warm Up

Work with a partner or in a group. Discuss the following questions.

1. How often do you disagree with someone's opinion in a meeting?
2. Why is disagreeing important to a meeting?
3. How do you handle having someone disagree with you?

 Dialogue

Practice the dialogue with a partner.

> A: Let's discuss the Los Angeles branch. I think we should expand our business there.
>
> B: **I'm not sure that's the best approach.** If anything, we should scale back.
>
> A: Scale back? **I don't think that's a good idea.** We've invested too much money already.
>
> B: **I understand your point, but it's too risky.**
>
> A: Why do you think it's too risky?
>
> B: The market is too small for our products.
>
> A: **That's a good point.** How does the CEO feel about it?
>
> B: She doesn't think there is much potential there.

A: 우리 Los Angeles 지사에 대해 얘기를 해보죠. 그쪽 사업을 확장하면 좋을 것 같습니다.
B: 그게 가장 좋은 **방법**인지 잘 모르겠습니다. 오히려 축소하는 게 좋을 듯합니다.
A: 축소요? 그건 좋은 생각이 아닌 것 같습니다. 우리는 이미 너무 많은 돈을 투자했잖아요.
B: 무슨 말씀인지 알겠지만, 위험 부담이 너무 큽니다.
A: 왜 너무 위험할 거라고 생각하나요?
B: 우리 제품에 비해 시장이 너무 작아요.
A: **좋은 지적입니다.** CEO께서는 어떻게 생각하세요?
B: 그녀는 거기에 잠재력이 별로 없다고 생각하세요.

✓ Comprehension Check

Answer the questions.

1. What does the first speaker think they should do with the L.A. branch?
2. Why does the second speaker think it's too risky?

Vocabulary

Match the words or expressions with the correct definitions.

1. expand _____
2. approach _____
3. point _____
4. risky _____
5. potential _____

a. 지적
b. 위험한
c. 잠재력, 가능성
d. 확장하다
e. 접근법, 방법

⊕ Bonus Resources

keep in mind   ~을 명심하다, ~을 염두에 두다

A: **Keep in mind** that we signed the contract.
우리가 계약서를 체결했다는 걸 명심하세요.
B: That's a good point. 좋은 지적입니다.

keep in mind는 원가를 '머리에 유지하다'라고 직역이 되는데, 어떤 중요한 요점을 '명심하다', '염두에 두다'라는 뜻이다.

Grammar Points

Read the following and practice making sentences.

1. I'm not sure that's ~

> I'm not sure that's ~는 I don't think that's ~와 비슷한 뜻을 가졌지만 조금 더 정중하게 반대 입장을 말할 때 쓰는 패턴이다. 뒤에 동의하지 않는 점을 언급한다.
>
> 📖 *I'm not sure that's a viable option.* 실행 가능한 방법인지 잘 모르겠습니다.

a) I'm not sure that's the _____ solution. 맞는 해결책인지 잘 모르겠습니다.

b) I'm not sure that's a _____ assessment. 공정한 평가인지 잘 모르겠습니다.

c) I'm not sure that's the _____ alternative. 유일한 대안인지 잘 모르겠습니다.

2. I don't think that's ~

> I don't think that's ~는 상대방의 의견이나 제안에 반대 의사를 밝힐 때 유용한 패턴으로, 뒤에 반대하는 것을 언급하면 된다.
>
> 📖 *I don't think that's a relevant point.* 적절한 지적이 아닌 것 같습니다.

a) I don't think that's a _____ method. 좋은 방법이 아닌 것 같습니다.

b) I don't think that's the _____ approach. 맞는 접근법이 아닌 것 같습니다.

c) I don't think that's a _____ idea. 나쁜 생각이 아닌 것 같습니다.

✏ Write

Make your own dialogue using the expressions from Grammar Points.

A: _____

B: _____

 **Practice**

Shadowing

Listen and repeat.

1. **I'm not sure that's** the only answer.
   I'm not sure that's their motive.
2. **I don't think that's** the way to go.
   I don't think that's the point.
3. **I understand your** concern, **but** we should proceed.
   I understand your situation, **but** we have no choice.
4. **That's** a nice gesture.
   That's the right mindset.
5. Please **keep in mind** that we don't have much time.

Making Sentences

Practice making sentences. Use the words in the parentheses or use your own. Then, read your sentences to your partner or group. After sharing your sentences, practice saying someone else's sentences.

1. I'm not sure that's _____. (what, issue, response)
2. I don't think that's _____. (something, analogy)
3. I understand your point, but _____. (unrealistic, not relevant, not easy)
4. That's _____. (point, summary, truth)

 ## Roleplay

Roleplay the following scenarios with a partner. Practice and change roles.

Scenario 1

Two people are discussing a particular idea.
Person 1: suggest hiring more engineers
Person 2: say that you're not sure that is a good idea

Scenario 2

Meeting attendees are talking about a budget.
Person 1: suggest that they cut down on R&D budget for next year
Person 2: disagree and say why you think it's a bad idea

 ## Homework

Write a short dialogue of two people disagreeing about something.

_____

_____

_____

Warm Up Sample Answers
1. I (sometimes/never) disagree with someone's opinion in a meeting.
2. It's important because (it's constructive / it helps people find solutions to problems).
3. I (accept disagreements / get a little upset / really don't care).

Comprehension Check Answers
1. The first speaker suggests expanding their business there.
2. The second speaker thinks it's too risky because the market is too small for their products.

Vocabulary Answers
1. d, 2. e, 3. a, 4. b, 5. c

Grammar Points Answers
1. a) right b) fair c) only
2. a) good b) right c) bad

Write Sample Answer
A: I don't think that's a good idea.
B: I'm not sure that's a good idea, either.

Making Sentences Sample Answers
1. I'm not sure that's (what Joe said / an issue / a proper response).
2. I don't think that's (something we need to consider / a good analogy).
3. I understand your point, but (it's unrealistic / that's not relevant / that's not easy).
4. That's (a fair point / a good summary / the truth).

Roleplay Sample Answer
Scenario 1
Person 1: We should hire more engineers.
Person 2: I'm not sure that's a good idea.

Homework Sample Answer
Person 1: Maybe we should discountinue the product.
Person 2: I don't think that's a good idea. Keep in mind that it's still selling pretty well.
Person 1: That's a good point. But it's too expensive to produce.
Person 2: I understand your point, but that doesn't mean we should discontinue the product. In fact, we should increase production.
Person 1: What? I'm not sure that's the best approach.

> **Meeting Tip**

Feedback Should Be Constructive
피드백은 건설적이어야 한다

① **Focus on the problem, not the person.** 사람말고 문제에 집중해라.

When giving constructive feedback, do not mention the recipient's personal faults. Rather, discuss the work itself.

건설적인 피드백을 줄 때는 상대방의 개인적 결점에 대한 언급은 피한다. 대신 작업 자체에 대해 논의한다.

② **Discuss what can be improved, not what is wrong.** 틀린 것말고 개선할 수 있는 것을 논의해라.

Talk about the specific problems and how they can be improved.

특정적인 문제를 언급하면서 어떻게 개선할 수 있는지 말한다.

③ **Be specific, not general.** 보편적이지 말고 구체적이게 해라.

Don't be vague. Make sure the recipient knows what problems you're pointing out.

모호함을 피한다. 내가 어떤 문제점을 지적하고 있는지 상대방이 잘 알 수 있도록 한다.

④ **Confirm understanding.** 이해했음을 확실히 해라.

If you are uncertain the recipient understood your point, go ahead and ask for confirmation.

내가 지적하는 점들을 상대방이 이해했는지 확실치 않으면 가서 확인을 한다.

⑤ **Don't be defensive.** 방어적인 태도를 보이지 마라.

When receiving feedback, be open-minded. Avoid being defensive.

피드백을 받을 때는 열린 마음을 유지한다. 방어적인 태도는 피한다.

9 Deadlines and Schedules
When is the deadline for the sales report?

Learning Objectives

- Learners can discuss schedules and delays.
- Learners can talk about meeting deadlines.
- Learners can say how long a task will take to complete.

Warm Up

Work with a partner or in a group. Discuss the following questions.

1. Why do people make detailed schedules?
2. Do you have many deadlines to meet?
3. How often do you have to write reports?

Dialogue

Practice the dialogue with a partner.

A: Larry, are you done with the sales report?

B: Not yet. **There's been a delay.**

A: A delay? What kind of delay?

B: I just got the necessary data from the Busan store this morning. I need to add the data to the report.

A: **When is the deadline for the sales report?**

B: It's Friday next week. **We can still make the deadline.**

A: Are you sure?

B: Yes. **I just need a few more days to finish it.**

A: Larry, 판매 보고서는 마무리했나요?
B: 아직요. **지연이 생겼었어요.**
A: 지연이요? 무슨 지연이요?
B: 오늘 아침에 부산 매장에서 필요한 데이터를 겨우 받았어요. 그 데이터를 보고서에 포함해야 해서요.
A: **판매 보고서 마감일이 언제죠?**
B: 다음 주 금요일입니다. **아직 마감일을 맞출 수 있습니다.**
A: 확실해요?
B: 네. **끝내려면 며칠만 더 필요합니다.**

✓ Comprehension Check

Answer the questions.

1. What was the cause of the delay?
2. How much longer does Larry need to finish the sales report?

Vocabulary

Match the words or expressions with the correct definitions.

1. sales report _____
2. not yet _____
3. delay _____
4. deadline _____
5. still _____

a. 마감일, 마감 기한
b. 아직 (아니다)
c. 여전히
d. 판매 보고서, 세일즈 리포트
e. 지연

⊕ Bonus Resources

on track 착착 진행 중인

A: Are we **on track** with the report? 보고서는 잘 진행되고 있나요?
B: Absolutely. We can make the deadline. 그럼요. 마감일을 맞출 수 있어요.

on track은 원래 '선로 위에 있는'이라는 뜻으로, 어떤 일이 선로를 벗어나지 않고 '착착 진행 중' 이라는 말이다.

057

Grammar Points

Read the following and practice making sentences.

1. When is the ~?

> When is the ~?는 '~가 언제죠?'라며, 날짜를 물을 때 유용한 패턴으로 뒤에 명사가 따른다.
>
> 📖 *When is the next meeting?* 다음 회의가 언제죠?

    a) When is the _____ with the client? 고객과의 회의가 언제죠?
    b) When is the farewell _____ for Anna? Anna의 송별회가 언제죠?
    c) When is the delivery _____? 배달 날짜가 언제죠?

2. We can still ~

> We can still ~은 '뭔가를 하기에 아직 늦지 않았다'라는 의미가 있다. still 뒤에 할 수 있는 행위를 언급하면 된다.
>
> 📖 *We can still talk to them.* 아직 그들과 얘기할 수 있습니다.

    a) We can still _____ back. 아직 돌아갈 수 있습니다.
    b) We can still _____ the agreement. 아직 합의를 취소할 수 있습니다.
    c) We can still _____. 아직 기다릴 수 있습니다.

✏ Write

Make your own dialogue using the expressions from Grammar Points.

A: _____

B: _____

 **Practice**

Shadowing

Listen and repeat.

1. **There's been** an incident.
   There's been a change of plan.
2. **When is the** meeting?
   When is the next expo?
3. **We can still** turn in the report.
   We can still make a reservation.
4. **I just need** a few more minutes.
   I just need two more weeks to complete it.
5. Are we still **on track**?

Making Sentences

Practice making sentences. Use the words in the parentheses or use your own. Then, read your sentences to your partner or group. After sharing your sentences, practice saying someone else's sentences.

1. There's been _____. (incident, problem)
2. When is the _____? (meeting, deadline)
3. We can still _____. (tell, try, talk)
4. I just need _____. (hours, time, week)

Roleplay

Roleplay the following scenarios with a partner. Practice and change roles.

Scenario 1

Two people are talking about a deadline.
Person 1: ask Person 2 when the deadline for the report is
Person 2: reply that it's tomorrow and say that we can still make the deadline

Scenario 2

Two people are discussing if a deadline can be met.
Person 1: Ask Person 2 when the deadline for the proposal is and if we can make the deadline
Person 2: say you're almost done but need a few more days

Homework

Write a short dialogue of two people talking about a deadline.

Warm Up Sample Answers
1. Because detailed schedules (help people check their progress / can be shared with everyone).
2. (Yes, I have / No, I don't have) many deadlines.
3. I have to write reports once a week. / I rarely have to write reports.

Comprehension Check Answers
1. The Busan store sent the necessary data this morning.
2. Larry needs a few more days.

Vocabulary Answers
1. d, 2. b, 3. e, 4. a, 5. c

Grammar Points Answers
1. a) meeting b) party c) date
2. a) go b) cancel c) wait

Write Sample Answer
A: When is the deadline for the proposal?
B: It's on Friday. We can still make it.

Making Sentences Sample Answers
1. There's been (an incident at the factory / a problem with communication).
2. When is the (next meeting with them / deadline for the proposal)?
3. We can still (tell them no / try a different supplier / talk to the sales team).
4. I just need (a few more hours / some time to think / a week or so).

Roleplay Sample Answer
Scenario 1
Person 1: When is the deadline for the report?
Person 2: Tomorrow. We can still make the deadline.

Homework Sample Answer
Person 1: When is the deadline for the sales report?
Person 2: It's on March 2. I just need a few more days to finish it.
Person 1: I thought you were done.
Person 2: There's been a delay. I'm waiting for the data from our Daejeon office. But we're still on track. We can still make the deadline.

> **Meeting Tip**

Prepositions of Time
시간 전치사

특정 시간대	전치사	예문
요일	on	The meeting is **on** Monday. 회의는 월요일에 있습니다. I usually work from home **on** Thursdays. 보통 목요일에는 재택근무 합니다.
특정 날짜	on	The store opened **on** December 12. 12월 12일에 매장이 개장했습니다. The exhibition was held **on** March 5, 2023. 2023년 3월 5일에 전시회가 열렸습니다.
하루 중 시간대	at	The dinner is **at** 7 P.M. 저녁 식사는 저녁 7시입니다. I'll see you **at** noon. 정오에 뵙겠습니다. I usually go to bed **at** midnight. 보통 자정에 잡니다. I check my e-mails **at** night. 밤에 이메일을 확인해요.
오전, 오후, 저녁	in	I'll stop by **in** the morning. 오전에 들르겠습니다. The meeting is **in** the afternoon. 오후에 회의가 있습니다. I review my schedule **in** the evenings. 저녁에 일정을 검토합니다.
월, 년도, 계절	in	The deadline is **in** December. 마감일이 12월입니다. The company was founded **in** 1995. 회사는 1995년에 설립되었습니다. We update our business plan **in** the winter. 우리는 겨울에 사업 계획을 업데이트합니다.

10 Progress Report
Why don't you give us an update on the progress?

 ## Learning Objectives

- Learners can ask others for progress updates.
- Learners can explain what they are working on.
- Learners can ask if there are any challenges or issues to discuss.

 ## Warm Up

Work with a partner or in a group. Discuss the following questions.

1. Are progress meetings important?
2. What are some challenges you face at work?
3. Do you have to give updates to your supervisor often?

 ## Dialogue

Practice the dialogue with a partner.

> A: Okay, let's move on to the new product. Ben, **why don't you give us an update on the progress?**
>
> B: Well, we're ready to start production next week.
>
> A: That's great news. Are we getting a new website?
>
> B: Yeah. **We're currently working on the website.**
>
> A: Great. **Let's talk about any challenges that we're facing. Are there any issues that need to be addressed?**
>
> B: Yes. We need additional funds for marketing.
>
> A: I've already talked to the director about that. We should hear back from him this week.

A: 자, 신규 제품으로 넘어갑시다. Ben, **진행 상황에 대해 업데이트해 주시겠어요?**
B: 아, 다음 주에 생산을 시작할 준비가 됐습니다.
A: 정말 좋은 소식이네요. 새로운 홈페이지도 있을 건가요?
B: 네. **현재 홈페이지 작업을 하는 중입니다.**
A: 좋습니다. 우리가 직면하고 있는 문제들을 논의해 봅시다. 해결해야 할 쟁점들이 있나요?
B: 네. 마케팅을 위한 추가 자금이 필요합니다.
A: 이미 그 건에 대해 이사님과 논의했습니다. 이번 주 답변을 받을 수 있을 겁니다.

✓ Comprehension Check

Answer the questions.

1. When can they start production of the new product?
2. What does Ben say they need?

Vocabulary

Match the words or expressions with the correct definitions.

1. progress _____	a. 직면하다
2. work on _____	b. 문제
3. challenge _____	c. 진행 사항
4. face _____	d. 자금
5. funds _____	e. 작업하다

⊕ Bonus Resources

touch base 연락하다, 접촉하다

A: Let's talk about any new issues as they come up.
새로운 쟁점들이 생기는 대로 논의합시다.
B: Okay. Let's **touch base** at least once a week.
좋습니다. 적어도 매주 한번은 연락합시다.

touch base는 야구에서 베이스를 밟는다는 뜻인데, 비즈니스 상황에서는 '다시 연락하자'라는 의미다.

 **Grammar Points**

Read the following and practice making sentences.

1. We're currently + ~ing ~

> We're currently + ~ing ~는 '현재 뭔가를 하고 있다'는 뜻을 전할 때 쓰는 패턴이다.
> *We're currently assess*ing *the damage.* 현재 피해 상황을 파악하는 중입니다.

a) We're currently _____ for an answer. 현재 답을 찾는 중입니다.
b) We're currently _____ with the client. 현재 고객과 논의하는 중입니다.
c) We're currently _____ up the project. 현재 프로젝트를 마무리하는 중입니다.

2. Let's talk about ~

> Let's talk about ~은 어떤 화제에 대해 '논의하자'를 뜻하며, 뒤에 명사가 따른다.
> *Let's talk about the problem.* 문제에 대해 논의해 봅시다.

a) Let's talk about any _____ you might have. 질문이 있으면 논의해 봅시다.
b) Let's talk about your current _____. 현재 당신의 상황에 대해 논의해 봅시다.
c) Let's talk about the development _____. 개발 일정에 대해 논의해 봅시다.

Write

Make your own dialogue using the expressions from Grammar Points.

A: _____

B: _____

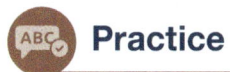

Practice

Shadowing

Listen and repeat.

1. **Why don't you** give us a summary?
   Why don't you show us the graphics?

2. **We're currently** finish**ing** up the design.
   We're currently work**ing** on it.

3. **Let's talk about** the new employee.
   Let's talk about something else.

4. **Are there any** issues?
   Are there any questions for me?

5. Can we **touch base** on Friday?

Making Sentences

Practice making sentences. Use the words in the parentheses or use your own. Then, read your sentences to your partner or group. After sharing your sentences, practice saying someone else's sentences.

1. Why don't you _____? (give, tell, ask)

2. We're currently _____. (talk, study, think)

3. Let's talk about _____. (benefits, topic, report)

4. Are there any _____? (issues, complaints)

 # Roleplay

Roleplay the following scenarios with a partner. Practice and change roles.

Scenario 1

Two people are talking about hiring new employees.

Person 1: ask Person 2 to give you an update

Person 2: say that you're currently interviewing candidates

Scenario 2

Two people are talking about problems with a project.

Person 1: ask if there are any problems

Person 2: say that you're currently experiencing many problems

 # Homework

Write a short dialogue of two people talking about the progress of a new product.

_____

_____

_____

Warm Up Sample Answers
1. (Yes, I / No, I don't) think so. / Maybe it's important for some teams.
2. I have many deadlines. / I have too much work.
3. Yes, I do. / No, I don't.

Comprehension Check Answers
1. They can start next week.
2. Ben says they need additional funds for marketing.

Vocabulary Answers
1. c, 2. e, 3. b, 4. a, 5. d

Grammar Points Answers
1. a) looking b) talking c) finishing
2. a) questions b) situation c) schedule

Write Sample Answer
A: We're currently experiencing some problems.
B: Let's talk about them.

Making Sentences Sample Answers
1. Why don't you (give us a briefing / tell us / ask the engineer)?
2. We're currently (talking to the workers / studying the risks / thinking about it).
3. Let's talk about (the benefits / a new topic / your report).
4. Are there any (outstanding issues / complaints about noise)?

Roleplay Sample Answer
Scenario 1
Person 1: Why don't you give us an update on the hiring status?
Person 2: I'm currently interviewing candidates.

Homework Sample Answer
Person 1: Why don't you give us an update on the progress of the new product?
Person 2: We're currently working on the website. We're also working on the product's slogan.
Person 1: Great. Let's talk about any challenges that we're facing. Are there any issues that need to be addressed?
Person 2: We're having trouble coming up with a slogan.
Person 1: Let me think of some ideas. Let's touch base tomorrow.

> **Meeting Tip**

Use Different Types of Listening for Different Situations
상황에 따라 여러 청취 방식을 사용하자

According to social scientists, there are many types of listening. Here are 3 types of listening that are useful in business situations.
사회 과학자들에 따르면 많은 청취 방식이 존재한다. 비즈니스 상황에서 유익한 3가지 방식을 소개한다.

① Informational Listening 정보성 듣기

You are simply focusing on what is being said. You are trying to comprehend and retain information. You are not making a judgment or evaluation of what you are hearing.
그저 상대방이 무슨 말을 하는지에 집중한다. 이해하고 정보를 유지하려고 노력한다. 듣는 것에 대해 판단이나 평가를 하지 않는다.

② Critical Listening 비판적 듣기

You are being critical of what is being said. You are trying to comprehend and evaluate the meaning. You are making judgments and agreeing or disagreeing with the speaker. If you do not agree, you should ask questions.
들리는 것에 대해 비판적이다. 이해하면서 평가를 하려고 한다. 판단을 하고 발언자와 동의하거나 반대한다. 동의하지 않으면 질문을 하는 것이 좋다.

③ Emphatic Listening 공감적 듣기

You are trying to comprehend what the speaker is thinking or feeling. You may or may not agree with what is being said. Be open-minded and civil. Allow the speaker to talk without interruption.
발언자가 어떤 생각을 하고 어떤 감정을 가지고 있는지 이해하려고 한다. 발언에 동의하거나 안 할 수 있다. 마음을 열고 예의를 지킨다. 발언자가 방해받지 않고 말을 할 수 있게 한다.

Zoom/WebEX Meeting Expressions

11 Can everyone hear me okay?

Learning Objectives

- **Learners can participate in a virtual meeting.**
- **Learners can check if others can see or hear them.**
- **Learners can ask questions or make requests during a virtual meeting.**

Warm Up

Work with a partner or in a group. Discuss the following questions.

1. How often do you have virtual meetings at work?
2. Do you speak much during these meetings?
3. How effective are most of the virtual meetings you attend?

Dialogue

Practice the dialogue with a partner.

> A: Hello, everyone. **Can everyone hear me okay?**
>
> B: I can't hear you, Linda. Wait. **You're on mute.** Do you see the button?
>
> A: Ah. Here we go. Ethan, can you hear me now? Hello?
>
> B: Loud and clear. Thanks.
>
> A: **Let me share my screen.** Can you all see the spreadsheet?
>
> B: You just had it. Now there's a photo of the product. **Could you bring up the spreadsheet again?**
>
> A: Let's see. Okay. Can you see it?
>
> B: Yes, I see it.

A: 모두 안녕하세요? **다들 제 말 들리나요?**
B: Linda, 안 들려요. 잠깐만요. **음소거가 되어 있네요.** 버튼 보이세요?
A: 아. 이거네요. Ethan, 이제 들려요? 여보세요?
B: 아주 잘 들립니다. 고마워요.
A: **저의 화면을 공유하겠습니다.** 다들 스프레드시트 보이시죠?
B: 방금 있었어요. 지금은 제품 사진이 보이고요. **스프레드시트 다시 띄우시겠어요?**
A: 어디 보자. 좋아요. 보이세요?
B: 네, 보입니다.

Comprehension Check

Answer the questions.

1. Why can't Ethan hear Linda?
2. What kind of document is Linda sharing?

Vocabulary

Match the words or expressions with the correct definitions.

1. on mute _____
2. loud and clear _____
3. share _____
4. spreadsheet _____
5. bring up _____

a. 올리다, 띄우다
b. 공유하다
c. 아주 분명하게
d. 음소거 되어있는
e. 스프레드시트

⊕ Bonus Resources

turn on/off 켜다/끄다

A: Can you hear me? 제 말 들려요?
B: Your sound is off. You have to **turn on** the sound.
   소리가 꺼진 상태입니다. 소리를 켜셔야 돼요.

turn on/off는 원래 무언가를 돌려서 켜고 끄는 걸 의미했지만 이제는 그저 뭐든 '켜다'와 '끄다'를 뜻할 때 사용한다.

Grammar Points

Read the following and practice making sentences.

1. Can everyone ~?

> Can everyone ~?은 한 사람이 아니라 함께 있는 모두에게 던지는 질문으로, 뭔가가 '가능한가?'라고 물을 때 쓰는 패턴이다.
>
> *Can everyone see the screen?* 다들 스크린 보이시나요?

a) Can everyone _____ the photograph? 다들 사진이 보이시나요?

b) Can everyone _____ my voice? 다들 제 목소리 들리시나요?

c) Can everyone _____ the graphics? 다들 도표가 이해되시나요?

2. Could you ~?

> Could you ~?는 '~을 할 수 있나?'를 뜻하며, 일상이나 비즈니스 상황에서 무엇을 요청할 때 매우 유용한 패턴이다. Can you ~?보다 더 격식을 차린 느낌을 주며, 뒤에 동사원형이 붙는다.
>
> *Could you speak up?* 더 크게 말씀하시겠어요?

a) Could you _____ me back? 다시 전화해 주시겠어요?

b) Could you _____ back to the last slide? 바로 전 슬라이드로 다시 가주시겠어요?

c) Could you _____ what you just said? 방금 언급하신 것 다시 말씀해 주시겠어요?

✍ Write

Make your own dialogue using the expressions from Grammar Points.

A: _____

B: _____

 **Practice**

Shadowing

Listen and repeat.

1. **Can everyone** hear the song?
   Can everyone understand the handwriting?

2. **You're** breaking up.
   You're on the screen.

3. **Let me** adjust the volume.
   Let me go back to the main slide.

4. **Could you** bring up the drawing again?
   Could you describe it?

5. Let me **turn on** the webcam.

Making Sentences

Practice making sentences. Use the words in the parentheses or use your own. Then, read your sentences to your partner or group. After sharing your sentences, practice saying someone else's sentences.

1. Can everyone _____? (see, hear, say)

2. You're _____. (good, not on)

3. Let me _____. (explain, adjust, get back)

4. Could you _____? (give, say, explain)

Roleplay

Roleplay the following scenarios with a partner. Practice and change roles.

Scenario 1

Participants are sharing information during a virtual meeting.

Person 1: ask if everyone can see your spreadsheet

Person 2: say you can't hear Person 1

Scenario 2

Two people are talking about problems during a virtual meeting.

Person 1: ask if everyone can see the spreadsheet

Person 2: say that the numbers are too small / suggest Person 1 read the data

Homework

Write a short dialogue of participants in a virtual meeting.

_____

_____

_____

Warm Up Sample Answers
1. I (often/sometimes/never) have virtual meetings at work.
2. Yes, I do. / No, I don't. / It depends on the type of meeting.
3. Usually, they are (not) effective.

Comprehension Check Answers
1. Because Linda is on mute.
2. Linda is sharing a spreadsheet.

Vocabulary Answers
1. d, 2. c, 3. b, 4. e, 5. a

Grammar Points Answers
1. a) see b) hear c) understand
2. a) call b) go c) repeat

Write Sample Answer
A: Can everyone see the chart?
B: Could you increase the screen size?

Making Sentences Sample Answers
1. Can everyone (see me / hear that / say their names)?
2. You're (good / not on the screen).
3. Let me (explain that / adjust the size / get back to you on that).
4. Could you (give us more details / say the number again / explain that)?

Roleplay Sample Answer
Scenario 1
Person 1: Can everyone see the spreadsheet?
Person 2: I can't hear you.

Homework Sample Answer
Person 1: Can everyone hear me okay?
Person 2: We can't hear you. You're on mute.
Person 1: Wait a minute. Let me turn on the sound. Okay. Let me share my screen. Do you see the spreadsheet?
Person 2: Yes. Oh, wait. Now it's gone. Could you bring up the spreadsheet again?

Meeting Tip

Basic Zoom Terminology and Features
기본적인 줌 용어 및 기능들

① **The Host** 호스트

The host schedules and manages the meeting.
호스트는 회의를 주최하고 관리한다.

② **Co-hosts** 공동 호스트

The host can assign a co-host during the meeting. A co-host shares most of the controls with the host.
회의 중에 호스트는 공동 호스트를 지정할 수 있다. 공동 호스트는 대부분의 호스트 통제 기능을 함께 쓴다.

③ **Guests (Participants)** 게스트

Guests are the participants who are invited to the meeting.
게스트는 회의에 초대된 참석자다.

④ **Share Screen** 화면 공유

The host's entire screen, specific apps, or whiteboard can be shared. The host can allow guests to share their screen also.
호스트의 전체 화면이나 특정 앱, 화이트보드를 공유할 수 있다. 호스트는 게스트에게도 화면 공유 권한을 줄 수 있다.

⑤ **Muting** 음소거

Guests can mute their own microphones. The host can also mute the microphones of guests.
게스트마다 마이크를 음소거 상태로 만들 수 있다. 호스트는 게스트의 마이크도 음소거 시킬 수 있다.

⑥ **Chat Window** 채팅창

Participants can send messages or files to others by using the Chat window.
참석자들은 채팅창을 통해 메시지나 파일을 다른 이들에게 보낼 수 있다.

12 — Zoom/WebEX Troubleshooting
My screen froze.

Learning Objectives

- **Learners can tell others how to use a virtual meeting app's features.**
- **Learners can explain what is wrong with their screen or sound.**
- **Learners can confirm that a problem has been remedied.**

Warm Up

Work with a partner or in a group. Discuss the following questions.
1. Do you normally get help from people when using a virtual meeting app's features?
2. In your opinion, what is the maximum number of people that can participate in a virtual meeting?
3. Are there some features that give you trouble frequently?

Dialogue

Practice the dialogue with a partner.

> A: Barry, I can't hear you. You have to turn off the mute button.
>
> B: I don't see it. Uh, where is it?
>
> A: **If you look at the tool bar, you'll see the mute button.**
>
> B: Okay. I see it. There. Andy, do you hear me now?
>
> A: Oh, now you're too loud. **Can you check your audio settings?**
>
> B: Sorry. I got it. Okay, now, how do I share my screen?
>
> A: **You have to click on the "Share Screen" button.**
>
> B: Okay. Wait. **My screen froze.** Wow, this is not easy.

A: Barry, 안 들려요. 음소거 버튼을 끄셔야 해요.
B: 안 보이는데요. 음, 어디 있죠?
A: **툴바를 보시면 음소거 버튼이 보이실 겁니다.**
B: 알겠어요. 보여요. 됐어요. Andy, 이제 들리나요?
A: 아, 이제 소리가 너무 큽니다. **오디오 설정을 한번 확인해 보시겠어요?**
B: 죄송해요. 됐네요. 좋아요, 이제 제 스크린을 어떻게 공유하죠?
A: **'스크린 공유' 버튼을 클릭하셔야 합니다.**
B: 알겠어요. 잠깐만요. **제 화면이 멈췄어요.** 와, 이거 쉽지 않네요.

✓ Comprehension Check

Answer the questions.

1. Who seems know more about the settings?
2. What happens to Barry's screen at the end?

Vocabulary

Match the words or expressions with the correct definitions.

1. button _____
2. too loud _____
3. setting _____
4. share _____
5. freeze _____

a. 설정
b. 공유하다
c. 소리가 너무 큰
d. 버튼
e. 멈추다, 얼다

⊕ Bonus Resources

turn up/down 높이다/낮추다

A: Can you check your sound? You're really loud.
음성 확인하시겠어요? 소리가 정말 커요.
B: I'll **turn** the sound **down**. 음성을 낮출게요.

turn up/down은 기기에서 나오는 소리를 '높이다'와 '낮추다'를 말할 때 쓰는 표현들이다.

 Grammar Points

Read the following and practice making sentences.

1. Can you check ~?

> Can you check ~?에서 check는 '확인하다'로 '~을 확인해 보시겠어요?'라는 뜻이다.
>
> 🖼 *Can you check the audio?* 음성을 확인해 보시겠어요?

    a) Can you check the _____? 음량을 확인해 보시겠어요?
    b) Can you check your _____? 웹캠을 확인해 보시겠어요?
    c) Can you check the _____? 앱을 확인해 보시겠어요?

2. You have to ~

> You have to ~는 '~을 해야 한다'를 뜻하며, 뒤에 상대방이 해야 하는 행위를 동사원형으로 붙인다.
>
> 🖼 *You have to update the app.* 앱을 업데이트하셔야 합니다.

    a) You have to _____ your mouse. 마우스를 연결하셔야 합니다.
    b) You have to _____ off your screen. 스크린을 꺼셔야 합니다.
    c) You have to _____ the settings. 설정을 확인하셔야 합니다.

⊘ Write

Make your own dialogue using the expressions from Grammar Points.

A: _____

B: _____

 **Practice**

Shadowing

Listen and repeat.

1. **If you look at** the webcam, you might see a cap over the camera.
   If you look at your monitor, you'll see a tool bar.

2. **Can you check** your mouse?
   Can you check the window?

3. **You have to** close the other windows.
   You have to minimize the window.

4. **My** screen turned black.
   My tool bar moved.

5. I'll **turn down** the sound.

Making Sentences

Practice making sentences. Use the words in the parentheses or use your own. Then, read your sentences to your partner or group. After sharing your sentences, practice saying someone else's sentences.

1. If you look at _____. (tool bar, Chat window)

2. Can you check _____? (keyboard, size)

3. You have to _____. (minimize, right-click)

4. My _____. (tool bar, screen)

Roleplay

Roleplay the following scenarios with a partner. Practice and change roles.

Scenario 1

> **Two people are talking about the "Share Screen" function.**
> **Person 1:** ask if Person 2 can see the screen
> **Person 2:** say that Person 1 needs to click on the "Share Screen" button

Scenario 2

> **Two people are having a virtual meeting.**
> **Person 1:** ask Person 2 how to use the menu
> **Person 2:** tell Person 1 to find the tool bar

Homework

Write a short dialogue of two people talking about various functions on Zoom or another virtual meeting app.

_____

_____

_____

Warm Up Sample Answers
1. I (don't) normally get help when using a virutal meeting app's features.
2. I think (3/5/10) is the maximum number. / I'm not sure.
3. Yes, there are. / No, there aren't. / I often forget to turn off the mute button.

Comprehension Check Answers
1. Andy seems to know more about the settings.
2. Barry's screen freezes.

Vocabulary Answers
1. d, 2. c, 3. a, 4. b, 5. e

Grammar Points Answers
1. a) volume b) webcam c) app
2. a) connect b) turn c) check

Write Sample Answer
A: Can you check your microphone?
B: It's not my microphone. You have to turn up your volume.

Making Sentences Sample Answers
1. If you look at (the tool bar, you'll see the "Whiteboard" button / the Chat window, you'll see where you can type your message).
2. Can you check (your keyboard / the window size)?
3. You have to (minimize the window / right-click the Zoom icon).
4. My (tool bar is gone / screen went blank).

Roleplay Sample Answer
Scenario 1
Person 1: Can you see the screen?
Person 2: Not yet. You have to click on the "Share Screen" button.

Homework Sample Answer
Person 1: I can't hear you very well. Can you check your audio settings?
Person 2: Okay, I'll turn up the volume. Now, how do I share my screen?
Person 1: You have to click on the "Share Screen" button.
Person 2: Got it. One more thing. How do I mute?
Person 1: If you look at the tool bar, you'll see the mute button.
Person 2: Okay. Oh, no. My screen froze.

> **Meeting Tip**

Become Better Prepared for Virtual Meetings
화상 회의를 위한 준비를 더 잘하자

① A leader's role is very important. 리더의 역할이 매우 중요하다.

There are limitations to virtual meetings. As the leader, recognize these limitations and plan ahead.

화상 회의에는 한계가 존재한다. 리더로서 이런 한계를 인식하고 미리 준비한다.

② Send out information beforehand. 정보를 미리 배포한다.

Distribute the necessary information before the meeting. That way, attendees can review the information and come prepared.

회의 전에 필요한 정보를 배포한다. 그러면 참석자들이 정보를 검토하고 준비가 된 상태로 참가할 수 있다.

③ Do more than give out information. 정보 공유보다 더한다.

Make sure that the virtual meeting does not become an information-sharing meeting.

화상 회의가 그저 정보 공유 회의가 되지 않도록 주의한다.

④ Encourage active participation. 적극적인 참여를 격려한다.

Attendees can become passive. Get individuals to contribute to the discussion and interact with others.

참석자들은 수동적이 될 수 있다. 개개인이 논의에 참여하고 다른 이들과 소통하도록 한다.

⑤ Stay focused. 집중한다.

It is easy to become distracted. As an attendee, focus on the discussion. Don't check your phone or work on something else.

집중력이 흐트러지기 쉽다. 참석자로서 논의에 집중하자. 전화를 확인하거나 다른 일을 하지 말자.

PAGODA
BUSINESS
BIBLE

Basic

WRITING

1 Starting an E-mail

 Learning Objectives

- Learners can write a clear subject line.
- Learners can address the recipient correctly.
- Learners can write a formal greeting.

 Warm Up

Work with a partner or in a group. Discuss the following questions.

1. How many e-mails do you send per week?
2. Who sends you the most e-mails?
3. Do you prefer to communicate by e-mail or in person?

 **Structure**

E-mails consist of a title, body, closing statement, and sign-off.

이메일의 구성 요소	
발신자	▶ Make sure to use a professional e-mail account. 반드시 업무용 이메일 계정을 사용한다. *From: j.booker@wollainc.com* 발신: j.booker@wollainc.com
수신자	▶ Write the recipient's e-mail address. 받는 사람의 이메일 주소를 적는다. *To: h.boeman@wollainc.com* 수신: h.boeman@wollainc.com
제목	▶ Clearly indicate the subject of your e-mail. 이메일의 주제를 명확하게 명시한다. *Subject: Welcome to Wolla Inc.!* 제목: Wolla 사에 오신 것을 환영합니다!
인사, 용건	▶ Use an appropriate greeting depending on your relationship with the recipient. 수신자와의 관계에 따라 적절한 인사말을 사용한다. ▶ Use "Hi" if you are familiar with the recipient and are friendly with the person. Use "Dear" if you are contacting the recipient for the first time or if it is necessary to be more formal and polite. 수신자와 친분이 있는 경우 'Hi'를 사용한다. 처음 연락하는 사이이거나 좀 더 격식 있고 정중해야 할 경우에는 'Dear'를 사용한다. ▶ Introduce yourself, if necessary. 필요한 경우 자신을 소개한다. ▶ State the purpose of your e-mail clearly at the beginning of your message. 이메일의 목적을 메시지 첫머리에 명확하게 명시한다. *Dear Haley,* 안녕하세요, Haley. *How are you? I'm Jay Booker from the HR department. Welcome to Wolla Inc.!* 안녕하세요? 저는 인사팀의 Jay Booker입니다. Wolla 사에 입사하신 것을 환영합니다!
본문	▶ Add details that are relevant to the purpose of your e-mail. 이메일의 목적과 관련된 세부 정보를 추가한다. *It's so great to have you here.* 이곳에 오셔서 정말 반갑습니다. *If you need help in any way, let me know.* 뭐든지 도움이 필요하시면 언제든지 알려주세요.
마무리 인사	▶ Close with a proper sign-off. "Best regards" or "Regards" is commonly used in business e-mails. Use "Sincerely" if you want to sound more formal. 적절한 사인으로 마무리한다. 'Best regards'나 'Regards'는 비즈니스 이메일에 주로 사용된다. 좀 더 격식 있는 느낌을 주려면 'Sincerely'를 쓴다. ▶ Include your full name, position/title, and company name in more formal e-mails. 더 격식을 차려야 하는 이메일에서는 본인의 이름, 직책, 소속 회사를 포함한다. *Best regards,* 존경을 담아, *Jay Booker* Jay Booker *HR Specialist Wolla Inc.* HR 전문가 Wolla 사

 **Sample Writing**

Read the sample e-mail.

From: n.sanders@foxlitenews.org
To: j.powell@foxlitenews.org
Subject: Miller Project Meeting

Hi John,

Do you have time for a quick chat tomorrow? We need to discuss the Miller project. **Would Friday at 10 A.M. work for you?** Let me know as soon as you can.

Regards,

Naomi

발신: n.sanders@foxlitenews.org
수신: j.powell@foxlitenews.org
제목: Miller 프로젝트 회의

안녕하세요, John.

내일 잠깐 얘기할 시간이 있으신가요? Miller 프로젝트에 대해 논의할 게 있어요. 금요일 오전 10시 괜찮으시겠어요? 되도록 빨리 알려주세요.

존경을 담아,

Naomi

Comprehension Check

Answer the questions.

1. What does Naomi want to discuss with John?
2. When does Naomi want to meet John?

Vocabulary

Match the words or expressions with the correct definitions.

1. have time for _____
2. a quick chat _____
3. need to _____
4. work for _____
5. let me know _____
6. as soon as you can _____

a. ~에게 괜찮다
b. 되도록 빨리
c. ~할 시간 있다
d. 잠깐 얘기, 짧은 대화
e. ~해야 한다
f. 알려주세요

✓ Vocab Test

Fill in the blanks with the correct words or expressions.

have time for / a quick chat / need to / work for / let me know / as soon as you can

1. You _____ call her.
2. Let's have _____.
3. Text him _____.
4. We _____ some coffee.
5. _____ what you think.
6. Would this _____ you?

⊕ Bonus Resources

a while 한동안

A: Hi, Joe. It's good to see you. 안녕하세요, Joe. 정말 반가워요.
B: It's good to see you too. It's been **a while**. 저도 반가워. 오랜만입니다.

a while은 '한동안'을 뜻한다. 참고로 한 단어로 된 awhile은 '잠시'를 뜻하므로 a while과 뉘앙스가 다르다.

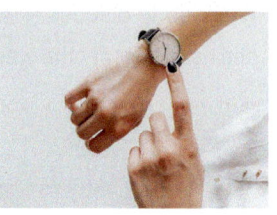

 ## Grammar Points

Read the following and practice making sentences.

1. Do you have time for ~?

> Do you have time for ~?는 '~을 위해 시간이 있나요?'라는 뜻으로, 무언가를 위해 할애할 시간이 있는지 묻는 것이다. 뒤에는 사람, 사물, 활동 등이 따른다.
>
> ➭ *Do you have time for a quick snack?* 간단한 간식을 드실 시간이 있나요?

    a) Do you have time for _____? 커피 한잔하실 시간 있어요?
    b) Do you have time for _____? 회의하실 시간 있어요?
    c) Do you have time for _____? 영화 보실 시간 있어요?

2. Would ~ work for you?

> Would ~ work for you?는 '(시간, 날짜 등)이 괜찮나요?'라는 뜻이다. 일정을 잡을 때 유용하게 쓸 수 있는 표현이다. 날짜나 요일 뒤에 시간도 언급할 때는 at + (시간) 형태로 쓴다.
>
> ➭ *Would Friday at 4 P.M. work for you?* 금요일 오후 4시 괜찮으세요?

    a) Would _____ work for you? 3월 15일 괜찮으세요?
    b) Would _____ work for you? 화요일 오후 2시 괜찮으세요?
    c) Would _____ work for you? 오전 10시 괜찮으세요?

 ## Practice

Making Sentences

Practice writing sentences. Use the given words or use your own. Then, read your sentences to your partner or group.

1. We need to discuss ~

    (the next project / the weekly budget / the plan)

- _____
- _____
- _____

2. ~ as soon as you can.

    (Tell me / Call me / Contact him)

- _____
- _____
- _____

Editing Sentences

Find a mistake in the e-mail and correct it.

> From: leilasmith@abccorp.com
> To: chavez70@abccorp.com
> Subject: June Meeting
>
> ①Hi Monica,
>
> Do you have time ②to a meeting after lunch? We need ③to discuss the budget for June. Would 1 P.M. work ④for you? Let me know.
>
> ⑤Best regards,
>
> Leila

 ## Real Writing

Write an e-mail based on the following scenarios. Exchange your e-mail with a partner and check your partner's e-mail for errors.

Scenario 1

> Write an e-mail to your coworker, Patty. Ask her if she has time for a phone call at 3 P.M. next Tuesday. You need to discuss an important project.

Scenario 2

> Write an e-mail to your boss, Mr. Wang. Ask your boss if he has time to talk about next month's budget report.

From: roha.rose@xyzcorp.com
To: patty.johnson@xyzcorp.com
Subject: _____

_____

_____

_____

Homework

Write a short business e-mail asking if the recipient has time for a quick chat.

Warm Up Sample Answers
1. I send (10 e-mails / one e-mail) per week.
2. My (biggest client / boss) sends me the most e-mails.
3. I prefer to communicate by e-mail because (I can plan what I want to say / it's very convenient).

Comprehension Check Answers
1. Naomi wants to discuss the Miller project with John.
2. Naomi wants to meet John on Friday at 10 A.M.

Vocabulary Answers
1. c, 2. d, 3. e, 4. a, 5. f, 6. b

Vocab Test Answers
1. need to, 2. a quick chat, 3. as soon as you can, 4. have time for, 5. Let me know, 6. work for

Grammar Points Answers
1. a) a cup of coffee b) a meeting c) a movie
2. a) March 15 b) Tuesday at 2 P.M. c) 10 A.M.

Editing Sentences Answer
② to → for

Real Writing Sample Answer
Scenario 1
Subject: Phone Call at 3 P.M. next Tuesday

Hi Patty,

Do you have some time for a quick phone call next Tuesday? We need to discuss an important project. Would 3 P.M. work for you? Let me know.

Regards,

Roha

Homework Sample Answer
Subject: Quick Chat Next Week

Hi Harry,

Do you have time for a quick chat next week? It's been a while. Would November 10 work for you? Let me know.

Regards,

Rebecca

Writing Tip

Instant Messaging Etiquette in Business
비즈니스 메신저 에티켓

① Say hello first. 인사부터 한다.

Begin with a casual greeting like "hello" or "hi." Then ask if the other person has time for a quick chat.

'Hello'나 'Hi' 같은 격식 없는 인사로 시작한다. 그런 다음 간단하게 대화할 시간이 있는지 묻는다.

② Make it short. 짧게 한다.

Use instant messaging for only short interactions. The other person should be able to respond quickly to your question or request. If not, send an e-mail instead.

메신저는 짧은 대화에만 쓴다. 나의 질문이나 요청에 상대방이 바로 대응할 수 있어야 한다. 아니라면 대신 이메일을 사용한다.

③ Avoid informal online abbreviations. 비격식 온라인용 약어는 삼간다.

In business situations, avoid informal abbreviations such as "LOL" (laugh out loud) or "CU" (see you). Use only well-established business abbreviations such as "FYI" (for your information) and "ASAP" (as soon as possible).

비즈니스 상황에서는 'LOL'(ㅋㅋ)이나 'CU'(안녕) 등 비격식 온라인용 약어를 삼간다. 확실한 'FYI'(참고로)와 'ASAP'(가능한 한 빨리) 같은 비즈니스 약어만 쓴다.

④ Discuss only simple topics. 간단한 주제만 다룬다.

Don't use instant messaging to discuss important issues and bad news. Use the phone or send an e-mail, or better yet, meet face-to-face.

중요한 문제나 나쁜 소식에 관한 논의는 메신저에서 피한다. 전화나 이메일을 사용하거나 대면하는 게 더 낫다.

⑤ End with a "thanks." 감사 인사로 마무리한다.

Make sure to close with a simple "thanks." You can also say "talk to you soon."

마무리할 때 간단한 "감사합니다"로 끝낸다. "또 연락해요"를 사용해도 된다.

2 Making Requests

 Learning Objectives

- Learners can make requests.
- Learners can use polite and respectful expressions for requests.
- Learners can express appreciation for the recipient's assistance.

 Warm Up

Work with a partner or in a group. Discuss the following questions.

1. Do you make many requests via e-mail?
2. Are most of your request e-mails to coworkers, vendors, or customers?
3. Why should routine e-mails be short?

Sample Writing

Read the sample e-mail.

From: pattyheart@paragon.com
To: mattvans@paragon.com
Subject: Need Feedback on Last Week's File

Hi Matt,

Could you check the file I sent you last week? It's a list of product ideas. I need to finalize it by Friday. **I would really appreciate it if you could give me some feedback on it.** Thanks!

Regards,

Patty

발신: pattyheart@paragon.com
수신: mattvans@paragon.com
제목: 지난주 파일에 대한 피드백이 필요해요

안녕하세요, Matt.

지난주 보내 드린 파일 확인해 주시겠어요? 제품 아이디어 목록입니다. 금요일까지 확정해야 합니다. **피드백을 좀 주시면 정말 감사하겠습니다.** 감사합니다!

존경을 담아,

Patty

Comprehension Check

Answer the questions.

1. What does Patty want Matt to do?
2. When did she send the list to Matt?

Vocabulary

Match the words or expressions with the correct definitions.

1. Could you _____
2. check _____
3. a list of _____
4. finalize _____
5. appreciate _____
6. feedback _____

a. 확정하다, 마무리 짓다
b. 고마워하다
c. 확인하다
d. ~하시겠어요
e. 피드백
f. ~의 목록

✓ Vocab Test

Fill in the blanks with the correct words or expressions.

Could you / check / a list of / finalize / appreciate / feedback

1. _____ call Pam?
2. Can you _____ something for me?
3. Let's _____ the schedule.
4. This is _____ our products.
5. I need your _____.
6. I _____ your help.

⊕ Bonus Resources

double-check 재확인하다

A: Can you **double-check** the numbers? 수치를 재확인해 주시겠어요?
B: Sure. 그러죠.

check가 한번 확인하는 것을 뜻하므로, 더블, 즉 '두 배'를 말하는 double이 들어가는 double-check는 '다시 한번 확인하다'가 된다.

 **Grammar Points**

Read the following and practice making sentences.

1. Could you check ~?

> Could you check ~?는 '~을 확인해 주시겠어요?'라고 물을 때 쓴다. Could 대신 Can을 쓸 수 있으나, Could가 조금 더 정중한 표현이다. 뒤에는 명사가 붙는다.
>
> 📧 *Could you check my e-mail?* 제 이메일 확인해 주시겠어요?

a) Could you check _____? 당신 시계를 확인해 주시겠어요?

b) Could you check _____? 데이터를 확인해 주시겠어요?

c) Could you check _____? 수정된 보고서를 확인해 주시겠어요?

2. I would really appreciate it if you could ~

> 다소 길게 느껴질 수 있는 이 패턴은 '~해 주시면 정말 고맙겠습니다'를 뜻한다. 뒤에는 상대방이 했으면 하는 행동을 동사로 붙인다.
>
> 📧 *I would really appreciate it if you could call me tomorrow.* 내일 전화 주시면 정말 고맙겠습니다.

a) I would really appreciate it if you could _____ with me.
   저와 함께 가주시면 정말 고맙겠습니다.

b) I would really appreciate it if you could _____ me.
   말씀해 주시면 정말 고맙겠습니다.

c) I would really appreciate it if you could _____ with her.
   그녀와 만나 주시면 고맙겠습니다.

Practice

Making Sentences

Practice writing sentences. Use the given words or use your own. Then, read your sentences to your partner or group.

1. It's ~
   (a memo / project photos / the revised report)

   -
   -
   -

2. I need to ~
   (forward it / take a look / think)

   -
   -
   -

Editing Sentences

Find a mistake in the e-mail and correct it.

From: jdjang@abccorp.com
To: blee@abccorp.com
Subject: New Cover Design

Hi Beth,

Can you ①check the attached cover design? It's the revised one. I need ②to give the designer our feedback on Friday. I ③would really appreciate ④you if you could ⑤take a look. Thanks!

Regards,

J.D.

 **Real Writing**

Write an e-mail based on the following scenarios. Exchange your e-mail with a partner and check your partner's e-mail for errors.

Scenario 1

> Write an e-mail to your coworker, Earl. Ask him to check the file you sent last week. It's a product list from Penn Inc. Say you'd appreciate it if he took a look at it this week.

Scenario 2

> Write an e-mail to your boss. Ask if your boss could meet with you tomorrow. Say it's urgent and you need to talk about the project.

From: kenoh@paragon.com
To: earlhanson@paragon.com
Subject: _____

_____
_____
_____

Homework

Write a short business e-mail requesting for the recipient to double-check the calculations.

_____
_____
_____

Warm Up Sample Answers
1. (Yes, I / No, I don't) make many requests via e-mail.
2. Most of my request e-mails are to (coworkers/vendors/customers).
3. They should be short because (they should be direct / people are busy / they are routine).

Comprehension Check Answers
1. She wants Matt to give her some feedback on a list of ideas.
2. She sent it last week.

Vocabulary Answers
1. d, 2. c, 3. f, 4. a, 5. b, 6. e

Vocab Test Answers
1. Could you, 2. check, 3. finalize, 4. a list of, 5. feedback, 6. appreciate

Grammar Points Answers
1. a) your (watch/clock) b) the data c) the revised report
2. a) go/come b) tell c) meet

Editing Sentences Answer
④ you → it

Real Writing Sample Answer
Scenario 1
Subject: Please Check Last Week's File

Hi Earl,

Could you check the file I sent you last week? It's a product list from Penn Inc. I would really appreciate it if you could take a look at it this week. Thanks.

Regards,

Ken

Homework Sample Answer
Subject: My Calcs Need Double-checking

Hi Carl,

Could you double-check my calculations? I need to send them to the sub tomorrow. I would really appreciate it if you could verify the numbers. Thanks!

Regards,

Paul

Writing Tip

Tips on Making Routine Requests
일상적인 요청 시 유용한 팁

① Open with your request. 요청으로 시작한다.

In general, it's good to use the direct approach. State your request at the beginning. Be clear and specific. Remember to use a polite tone. Don't be demanding.

통상적으로 단도직입적으로 접근하는 것이 좋다. 시작 부분에서 요청 자체를 언급한다. 명확하고 확실해야 한다. 예의 바른 어조를 쓰는 것을 기억한다. 과도하게 요구하는 느낌은 피한다.

EX **Formal** 격식 차림
I'm writing to request ~   ~을 위해 메일 드립니다.

Casual 격식 없는
Could you ~? / Would you mind + ~ing?   ~할 수 있나요? / ~해 주시겠어요?

② Say why you're making the request. 왜 요청하는지 언급한다.

Explain the reason for the request. Say why it's important. If possible, mention how the recipient will benefit from fulfilling your request.

요청하는 이유를 설명한다. 왜 중요한지 말한다. 가능하다면 상대방이 나의 요청을 들어주면 얻을 수 있는 이득을 언급한다.

EX **Formal** 격식 차림
I have been asked to ~ / I am required to ~   ~해달라는 요청을 받았습니다. / 저는 ~할 것을 요구받았습니다.

Casual 격식 없는
I need to ~ / I have to ~   ~해야 합니다. / ~해야 합니다.

③ Close with courtesy. 공손하게 마무리한다.

If there is a deadline, make sure to mention it. Include any contact information the recipient might need. Finally, end by saying you appreciate the recipient's assistance.

마감 기한이 있다면 확실히 언급한다. 상대방이 필요할 법한 연락처도 포함한다. 상대방의 도움에 대한 감사의 뜻을 전하면서 마무리한다.

EX **Formal** 격식 차림
Your assistance in ~ would be greatly appreciated. / Thank you in advance for your ~
~에 대한 도움을 주실 수 있으면 감사하겠습니다. / ~에 미리 감사를 드립니다.

Casual 격식 없는
Could you help me out with ~? / Thanks!   ~을 도와주시겠어요? / 감사합니다!

3 Scheduling a Meeting

Learning Objectives

- Learners can make requests to schedule a meeting.
- Learners can use professional language when scheduling a meeting.
- Learners can ask if the proposed date and time are convenient for the recipient.

Warm Up

Work with a partner or in a group. Discuss the following questions.
1. What communication method do you usually use when scheduling meetings?
2. How many times a month do you schedule meetings with clients or business partners?
3. In general, do you get a quick response to this type of e-mail?

Sample Writing

Read the sample e-mail.

From: pattyheart@paragon.com
To: sbullock@goodagency.com
Subject: Could we meet on Wednesday?

Dear Ms. Bullock,

I was wondering if I could schedule a meeting with you. It's about the new project in Saipan. Could we meet this Wednesday at 3 P.M.? **Please let me know if the proposed date and time work for you.**

Sincerely,

Patty Heart

발신: pattyheart@paragon.com
수신: sbullock@goodagency.com
제목: 수요일에 만날 수 있나요?

안녕하세요, Bullock님.

만나 뵐 수 있는 날짜를 잡을 수 있을까 해서요. 신규 Saipan 프로젝트 건입니다. 수요일 오후 3시에 만날 수 있을까요? 제 안해 드린 날짜와 시간이 괜찮으신지 말씀해 주세요.

존경을 담아,

Patty Heart

Comprehension Check

Answer the questions.

1. What does Patty want to do?
2. When does she propose that they meet?

Vocabulary

Match the words or expressions with the correct definitions.

1. wonder _____
2. schedule _____
3. about _____
4. proposed _____
5. date and time _____
6. work _____

a. 궁금하다
b. 제안된
c. ~에 관한
d. 일정을 잡다
e. 괜찮다, 가능하다
f. 날짜와 시간

✓ Vocab Test

Fill in the blanks with the correct words or expressions.

wondering / schedule / about / proposed / date and time / work

1. Do you know the _____ of the party?
2. Let's _____ a meeting.
3. The _____ date is April 2.
4. I'm _____ why he called.
5. That idea will _____ perfectly.
6. It's _____ the report.

⊕ Bonus Resources

on the same page 동의하는, 공감하는

A: Are we **on the same page** on the new date? 새 날짜에 동의하는 거죠?
B: Yes. I think December 1 is fine. 네. 12월 1일 좋을 것 같습니다.

on the same page는 마치 나와 상대방이 같은 페이지를 보고 있는 것처럼 무엇에 대해 '동의하는, 공감하는'을 뜻한다.

Grammar Points

Read the following and practice making sentences.

1. **I was wondering if I could ~**

> I was wondering은 '~이 궁금하다', if I could는 '내가 ~할 수 있는지'를 뜻한다. 합해서 I was wondering if I could ~는 '제가 ~할 수 있을까 해서요'라는 정중한 표현이 된다. 뒤에는 동사가 붙는다.
>
> 📖 *I was wondering if I could borrow your pen.* 펜을 좀 빌려도 될까 해서요.

a) I was wondering if I could _____ you a question. 질문 하나 드릴 수 있을까 해서요.

b) I was wondering if I could _____ now. 지금 갈 수 있을까 해서요.

c) I was wondering if I could _____ early. 일찍 퇴근할 수 있을까 해서요.

2. **Please let me know if ~**

> Please let me know if ~는 '~이 가능한지 알려 주세요'로, 뒤에 주어+동사가 붙는다. 친한 사이라면 Please를 생략할 수도 있다.
>
> 📖 *Please let me know if that's okay.* 그게 괜찮은지 알려 주세요.

a) Please let me know if _____ could go. 가실 수 있는지 알려 주세요.

b) Please let me know if _____ is ready. 보고서가 완성됐는지 알려 주세요.

c) Please let me know if _____ can attend. 당신 팀이 참석 가능한지 알려 주세요.

Practice

Making Sentences

Practice writing sentences. Use the given words or use your own. Then, read your sentences to your partner or group.

1. It's about ~

   (your director / the project / my company)

   * _____
   * _____
   * _____

2. Could we meet ~?

   (on the weekend / tomorrow / next week)

   * _____
   * _____
   * _____

Editing Sentences

Find a mistake in the e-mail and correct it.

From: briche@abccorp.com
To: mharris@abccorp.com
Subject: Are You Available Tomorrow?

Hi Mitch,

I ①<u>been</u> wondering if I could schedule a quick meeting ②<u>with</u> you. Could ③<u>we</u> meet tomorrow at 10 A.M.? Please let me ④<u>know</u> if the time ⑤<u>works</u> for you.

Regards,

Ben

Real Writing

Write an e-mail based on the following scenarios. Exchange your e-mail with a partner and check your partner's e-mail for errors.

Scenario 1

> Write an e-mail to Mindy, a co-worker. Ask her if you can meet her tomorrow at 2 P.M. Say it's about the new schedule.

Scenario 2

> Write an e-mail to a client. Ask if you can visit him sometime next week. Say it's about the recent order.

From: kharris@paragon.com
To: mkim@paragon.com
Subject: _____

_____
_____
_____

Homework

Write a short e-mail to schedule a meeting.

_____
_____
_____

Warm Up Sample Answers
1. I usually use (e-mail / the phone / text messages).
2. I schedule meetings (once / twice / several times) a week. / I usually don't schedule meetings with clients or business partners.
3. (Yes, I / No, I don't) usually get a quick response.

Comprehension Check Answers
1. She wants to meet with Ms. Bullock.
2. She proposes meeting on Wednesday at 3 P.M.

Vocabulary Answers
1. a, 2. d, 3. c, 4. b, 5. f, 6. e

Vocab Test Answers
1. date and time, 2. schedule, 3. proposed, 4. wondering, 5. work, 6. about

Grammar Points Answers
1. a) ask b) go c) leave
2. a) you b) the report c) your team

Editing Sentences Answer
① been → was

Real Writing Sample Answer
Scenario 1
Subject: Could we meet tomorrow?

Hi Mindy,

I was wondering if I could schedule a meeting with you. It's about the new schedule. Could we meet tomorrow at 2 P.M.? Please let me know if that's possible.

Regards,

Kit

Homework Sample Answer
Subject: Can we meet this Friday?

Hi Jonas,

I was wondering if I could schedule a meeting with you. Could we meet this Friday? We need to be on the same page on the project. Please let me know if that's possible.

Regards,

Toby

Writing Tip

Tips on Sending an E-mail to Schedule a Business Meeting
비즈니스 회의를 잡는 이메일을 보낼 때 유용한 팁

① Avoid Mondays and Fridays. 월요일과 금요일은 피한다.

Mondays are not recommended, because people are just returning from the weekend. Fridays are bad too, because people are getting ready for the weekend. Also, some people use personal days on Monday and Friday.

사람들이 주말을 막 마치고 돌아오기 때문에 월요일은 좋지 않다. 사람들이 주말을 준비하고 있는 금요일 역시 좋지 않다. 또한 월요일과 금요일은 휴가를 쓰는 이들이 있다.

② Go for the middle. 중간 요일에 잡는다.

The best days are Tuesday, Wednesday, and Thursday. People are generally in work mode. Out of the three days, Tuesday might be the best. This is because people can agree on tasks on Tuesday, and then they can work on their tasks throughout the week.

가장 좋은 날은 화요일과 수요일, 목요일이다. 이때 전반적으로 사람들이 업무 모드에 들어가 있다. 3일 중 화요일이 최적일 수 있다. 화요일에 할 업무에 대해 합의해서 그 주 내내 그 업무를 진행할 수 있기 때문이다.

③ Think in terms of parts of the day. 하루를 시간대로 생각한다.

Early Morning (9 A.M. – 10 A.M.) 이른 아침 (오전 9시 – 10시)
Mid-Morning (10 A.M. – noon) 오전 중반 (오전 10시 – 정오)
Lunchtime (12 P.M. – 1 P.M.) 점심시간 (오후 12시 – 1시)
Early Afternoon (1 P.M. – 3:30 P.M.) 이른 오후 (오후 1시 – 3시 30분)
Late Afternoon (3:30 P.M. – 5 P.M.) 늦은 오후 (오후 3시 30분 – 5시)
Evening (5 P.M. – 9 P.M.) 저녁 (오후 5시 – 9시)

4   Agreeing to a Request for a Meeting

 Learning Objectives

- Learners can confirm the receipt of a request for a meeting.
- Learners can agree to the meeting request.
- Learners can confirm the time and date of the meeting.

 Warm Up

Work with a partner or in a group. Discuss the following questions.

1. Do you get many e-mails requesting a meeting?
2. How often do you have to meet with clients or vendors in a month?
3. What do you usually discuss when you meet with a client or vendor?

Sample Writing

Read the sample e-mail.

From: a.patterson@abcok.com
To: jackpark@paragon.com
Subject: RE: Request for a Meeting

Hi Jack,

Thanks for your e-mail. **I'd be happy to have a meeting with you. March 15 sounds good.** I'll have the drawings ready. I'll see you at my office at 3 P.M.

Regards,

Amy

발신: a.patterson@abcok.com
수신: jackpark@paragon.com
제목: RE: 만남 요청

안녕하세요, Jack.

이메일 감사합니다. **당신과 기꺼이 만나겠습니다. 3월 15일 아주 좋습니다.** 도면은 준비해 놓겠습니다. 제 사무실에서 오후 3시에 뵙겠습니다.

인사를 전하며,

Amy

Comprehension Check

Answer the questions.

1. Can Amy have a meeting with Jack on March 15?
2. Where are they meeting?

Vocabulary

Match the words or expressions with the correct definitions.

1. I'd _____
2. be happy to _____
3. sound _____
4. drawing _____
5. ready _____
6. office _____

a. ~을 기꺼이 하다
b. 준비가 된
c. 나는 ~할 것이다 (I would의 축약형)
d. ~한 듯하다
e. 도면
f. 사무실

✓ Vocab Test

Fill in the blanks with the correct words or expressions.

> I'd / am happy to / sounds / drawings / ready / office

1. Come to my _____.
2. Are those the project _____?
3. _____ prefer to meet in the afternoon.
4. The meeting room will be _____ by then.
5. I _____ help.
6. Lunch _____ good.

⊕ Bonus Resources

drop someone a line ~에게 간단히 연락하다

A: If you have any questions, feel free to **drop me a line**.
   질문이 있으시면 언제든 연락주세요.
B: Thank you, I will. 감사합니다. 연락드리겠습니다.

drop someone a line은 누군가에게 간단한 메시지를 보내거나 짧게 연락하는 것을 의미하며, 일상적이면서 비격식적인 표현이다. 이 표현은 주로 이메일이나 문자 메시지를 통해 간단히 소식을 전하고 싶을 때 사용된다.

Grammar Points

Read the following and practice making sentences.

1. I'd be happy to ~

> I would의 축약형인 I'd가 들어가는 I'd be happy to ~는 '나는 기꺼이 ~하겠다'를 뜻한다. 뒤에는 동사를 붙인다.
>
> 📖 *I'd be happy to* have a meeting with your staff. 당신 직원들과 기꺼이 만나겠습니다.

a) I'd be happy to _____ you. 기꺼이 전화 드리겠습니다.

b) I'd be happy to _____. 기꺼이 참가하겠습니다.

c) I'd be happy to _____ here. 기꺼이 여기서 기다리겠습니다.

2. ~ sounds good.

> ~ sounds good은 '~가 좋다'를 뜻하며, 복수 주어가 앞에 붙는 경우에는 sounds가 sound로 바뀐다는 점을 유의한다.
>
> 📖 *Coffee sounds good.* 커피 좋습니다.

a) _____ sounds good. 9월 좋습니다.

b) _____ sound good. 그 색깔들 좋습니다.

c) _____ sounds good. 그 날짜 좋습니다.

Practice

Making Sentences

Practice writing sentences. Use the given words or use your own. Then, read your sentences to your partner or group.

1. Thanks for your ~

    (e-mail yesterday / concern / interest in our products)

    - _____
    - _____
    - _____

2. I'll see you ~

    (at the conference / on Friday / at 4 P.M.)

    - _____
    - _____
    - _____

Editing Sentences

Find a mistake in the e-mail and correct it.

From: mriche@abccorp.com
To: bradlee@wolla.com
Subject: RE: Meeting with You and Sarah

Hi Brad,

Thanks for your e-mail. ①I'd be happy to have ②a meeting with you and Sarah. Friday ③at 10 A.M. sounds good ④on me. I'll see you ⑤at your office.

Regards,

Mitch

Real Writing

Write an e-mail based on the following scenarios. Exchange your e-mail with a partner and check your partner's e-mail for errors.

Scenario 1

> Write a reply e-mail to Yolanda, a supplier's rep. Agree to meet with her team next Tuesday. Say 4 P.M. sounds good to you.

Scenario 2

> Write a reply e-mail to Mr. Fendi, a potential vendor. Agree to meet with him on May 2 at 10 A.M.

From: kfisher@xyzcorp.com
To: yhamilton@wolla.com
Subject: _____

_____
_____
_____

Homework

Write a short e-mail to accept a request for a meeting.

_____
_____
_____

Warm Up Sample Answers
1. (Yes, I / No, I don't) get many e-mails requesting a meeting.
2. I have to meet with (clients/vendors) (once / twice / a few times) a month.
3. I usually discuss (price/schedule/projects/delivery/contracts).

Comprehension Check Answers
1. Yes, she can.
2. They are meeting at Amy's office.

Vocabulary Answers
1. c, 2. a, 3. d, 4. e, 5. b, 6. f

Vocab Test Answers
1. office, 2. drawings, 3. I'd, 4. ready, 5. am happy to, 6. sounds

Grammar Points Answers
1. a) call b) attend c) wait
2. a) September b) (The/Those) colors c) That date

Editing Sentences Answer
④ on → to

Real Writing Sample Answer
Scenario 1
Subject: RE: Can we meet?

Hi Yolanda,

Thanks for your e-mail yesterday. I'd be happy to have a meeting with your team next Tuesday. 4 P.M. sounds good to me. See you then.

Regards,

Kurt

Homework Sample Answer
Subject: RE: Meet tomorrow at 2?

Dear Mr. Pitt,

Thanks for your e-mail. I'd be happy to meet with you. Tomorrow at 2 P.M. at your office sounds good to me. If you need anything, feel free to drop me a line.

Best regards,

Ken Fontaine

Writing Tip

Tips on Replying to Routine Requests
일상적인 요청에 답변할 때 유용한 팁

① Open with your answer to the request. 요청에 대한 답변으로 시작한다.

What the recipient wants to know is your answer. For this reason, you should state the answer right at the beginning. Make sure that it's clear and direct. Avoid giving unnecessary information.

상대방이 원하는 건 나의 답변이다. 그러니 답변을 바로 앞부분에 언급하는 것이 좋다. 명확하고 단도직입적이어야 한다. 불필요한 정보는 피한다.

Ex **Formal** 격식 차림
Regarding your request ~ / As you requested ~ / To answer your question ~
귀하의 요청과 관련해서 ~ / 요청하신 대로 ~ / 질문에 답변드리자면 ~

Casual 격식 없는
Sure. / Here is ~ 그렇게 하죠. / 여기 ~ 있습니다.

② Add details as needed. 필요한 세부 사항을 추가한다.

Provide any useful details or lists that support your answer. If your answer is negative, it may not be a good idea to give too much detail. However, if the relationship with the recipient is important, extra information may be necessary.

나의 답변을 뒷받침할 유용한 세부 사항이나 목록 등을 제공한다. 답변이 부정적이면 너무 많은 정보는 삼가는 것이 좋을 수 있다. 하지만 상대방과의 관계가 중요하다면 추가 정보가 필요할 수 있다.

Ex **Formal** 격식 차림
Unfortunately, ~ / Regrettably, ~ 유감스럽게도 ~ / 안타깝게도 ~

Casual 격식 없는
I want to ~ but ~ / But ~ ~하고 싶지만 / 하지만 ~

③ Close in a positive way. 긍정적으로 마무리한다.

Say "thank you" if appropriate. If the recipient needs to do something, let the person know what to do.

적절하다면 감사의 뜻을 밝힌다. 상대방이 해야 할 행동이 있다면 이를 알린다.

Ex **Formal** 격식 차림
I appreciate ~ / Please be advised that ~ ~에 감사드립니다. / ~을 숙지하시기를 바랍니다.

Casual 격식 없는
Thanks for ~ / Please ~ ~에 감사드려요. / ~하세요.

5 Rescheduling a Meeting

 Learning Objectives

- Learners can say they can't make the scheduled meeting with the recipient.
- Learners can ask to reschedule a meeting with the recipient.
- Learners can use appropriate expressions to apologize for the inconvenience.

 Warm Up

Work with a partner or in a group. Discuss the following questions.
1. Do you often have to reschedule meetings?
2. What are some of the reasons people might reschedule meetings?
3. Do other people often reschedule meetings with you?

Sample Writing

Read the sample e-mail.

From: jackpark@paragon.com
To: a.patterson@abcok.com
Subject: Need to Reschedule Our Meeting

Hi Amy,

Unfortunately, I won't be able to make next week's meeting. Could we reschedule for another day? I'm available all week the following week. I'm sorry for the inconvenience.

Regards,

Jack

발신: jackpark@paragon.com
수신: a.patterson@abcok.com
제목: 회의 일정 변경 필요

안녕하세요, Amy.

아쉽게도 다음 주 회의에 못 갈 거 같아요. 다른 날로 약속 변경할 수 있을까요? 그다음 주는 일주일 내내 시간이 됩니다. 불편을 끼쳐 죄송합니다.

인사를 전하며,

Jack

Comprehension Check

Answer the questions.

1. When was the meeting scheduled for?
2. When is Jack available?

Vocabulary

Match the words or expressions with the correct definitions.

1. unfortunately _____
2. won't _____
3. reschedule _____
4. another day _____
5. all week _____
6. the following week _____

a. 아쉽게도, 유감스럽게도
b. 다른 날
c. 그다음 주
d. ~ 못 할 것이다 (will not의 축약형)
e. 일주일 내내
f. 약속 일정을 변경하다

✓ Vocab Test

Fill in the blanks with the correct words or expressions.

unfortunately / won't / reschedule / another day / all week / the following week

1. Let's _____ the meeting.
2. He _____ tell me.
3. I'm free _____.
4. _____, I can't go.
5. Is it next week or _____?
6. We'll go _____.

⊕ Bonus Resources

short notice 갑작스러운 알림/통보

A: Can we go the following week? I'm sorry for the **short notice**.
그다음 주에 가도 될까요? 갑작스럽게 말씀드려 죄송합니다.

B: Sure, we can do that. 네, 그래도 돼요.

short notice는 직역하면 '짧은 통지'로, 뭔가를 너무 촉박하게, 갑작스럽게 알릴 때 쓰는 표현이다.

Grammar Points

Read the following and practice making sentences.

1. Unfortunately, I won't be able to ~

> Unfortunately, I won't be able to ~는 '나는 ~을 못 할 것 같다'를 뜻하며, 뒤에는 그 못하게 된 것을 동사로 붙인다. 참고로 won't는 will not의 축약형이다.
>
> *Unfortunately, I won't be able to attend.* 아쉽지만, 저는 참석 못 할 것 같습니다.

a) Unfortunately, I won't be able to _____ it.
아쉽지만, 저는 그걸 끝내지 못 할 것 같습니다.

b) Unfortunately, I won't be able to _____ the date.
아쉽지만, 저는 날짜를 바꾸지 못 할 것 같습니다.

c) Unfortunately, I won't be able to _____ the offer.
아쉽지만, 저는 제안을 수락 못 할 것 같습니다.

2. Could we reschedule for ~?

> Could we reschedule for ~?는 '~으로 약속 일정을 바꿀 수 있을까요?'를 묻는 패턴이다. 새로운 시간이나 날짜가 뒤에 붙는다. 좀 더 격식 없게 Could 대신 Can을 쓰기도 한다.
>
> *Could we reschedule for next week?* 다음 주로 약속을 변경할 수 있을까요?

a) Could we reschedule for _____? 오후 5시로 약속을 변경할 수 있을까요?

b) Could we reschedule for _____? 다음 달로 약속을 변경할 수 있을까요?

c) Could we reschedule for the _____ time? 더 이른 시간으로 약속을 변경할 수 있을까요?

 **Practice**

Making Sentences

Practice writing sentences. Use the given words or use your own. Then, read your sentences to your partner or group.

1. I'm available ~

   (tomorrow / this afternoon / now)

   • _____
   • _____
   • _____

2. I'm sorry for ~

   (the error / the phone call / making you wait)

   • _____
   • _____
   • _____

Editing Sentences

Find a mistake in the e-mail and correct it.

> From: sfernandez@mando.com
> To: robdelgado@tierra.com
> Subject: Can we reschedule the meeting?
>
> Hi Robert,
>
> ①Unfortunately, I ②won't be able to make the meeting on Friday. ③Could we reschedule ④in next Friday? I'm available ⑤all day. I'm sorry for the inconvenience.
>
> Regards,
>
> Steve

Real Writing

Write an e-mail based on the following scenarios. Exchange your e-mail with a partner and check your partner's e-mail for errors.

Scenario 1

> Write an e-mail to Yolanda, a supplier's rep. Say you can't make the meeting next Tuesday. Ask if you could reschedule for next Wednesday at 4 P.M.

Scenario 2

> Write an e-mail to a vendor. Say you can't make the meeting you have scheduled with the recipient. Ask if you could reschedule for a different date and time.

From: kfisher@xyzcorp.com
To: yhamilton@wolla.com
Subject: _____

_____
_____
_____

Homework

Write a short e-mail to reschedule a meeting.

_____
_____
_____

Warm Up Sample Answers
1. (Yes, I / No, I don't) often have to reschedule meetings.
2. They need to (attend to personal matters / meet with someone else / go see a doctor).
3. (Yes, they / No, they don't) often reschedule meetings with me.

Comprehension Check Answers
1. It was scheduled for next week.
2. He is available all week the following week.

Vocabulary Answers
1. a, 2. d, 3. f, 4. b, 5. e, 6. c

Vocab Test Answers
1. reschedule, 2. won't, 3. all week, 4. Unfortunately 5. the following week, 6. another day

Grammar Points Answers
1. a) finish b) change c) accept
2. a) 5 P.M. b) next month c) earlier

Editing Sentences Answer
④ in → for

Real Writing Sample Answer
Scenario 1
Subject: RE: Can we meet?

Hi Yolanda,

Unfortunately, I won't be able to make the meeting next Tuesday. Could we reschedule for next Wednesday at 4 P.M.? I'm sorry for the inconvenience.

Regards,

Kurt

Homework Sample Answer
Subject: RE: Meet tomorrow at 2?

Dear Mr. Pitt,

Unfortunately, I won't be able to make the meeting tomorrow. Could we reschedule for Friday at 2 P.M.? Please let me know. I'm really sorry about the short notice.

Regards,

Ken Fontaine

Writing Tip

Useful Expressions for Rescheduling Meetings
회의 일정 변경할 때 유용한 표현

① move 바꾸다

> Can we **move** our meeting to Friday? 우리 회의를 금요일로 바꿔도 될까요?
> Can we **move** our meeting to a different date? 우리 회의를 다른 날로 바꿔도 될까요?

② move up 앞당기다

> Can we **move** our meeting **up** to 10 A.M.? 우리 회의를 오전 10시로 앞당겨도 될까요?
> Can we **move** our meeting **up** an hour? 우리 회의를 한 시간 앞당겨도 될까요?

③ push back 늦추다

> Can we **push** our meeting **back** to 2 P.M.? 우리 회의를 오후 2시로 늦춰도 될까요?
> Can we **push** our meeting **back** an hour? 우리 회의를 한 시간 늦춰도 될까요?

④ postpone 연기하다

> Could we **postpone** our meeting to next week? 우리 회의를 다음 주로 연기해도 될까요?
> Could we **postpone** our meeting to 11 A.M.? 우리 회의를 오전 11시로 연기해도 될까요?

⑤ something came up 일이 생겼다

> **Something came up**, and I can't make it on Friday. 일이 생겨서 금요일 못 갈 것 같습니다.
> **Something** urgent **came up** that I need attend to. 처리해야 할 급한 일이 생겼습니다.

6 Congratulating Someone

Learning Objectives

- Learners can congratulate the recipient.
- Learners can specify what they are congratulating the recipient for.
- Learners can wish the recipient further success.

Warm Up

Work with a partner or in a group. Discuss the following questions.

1. What can you congratulate coworkers, clients, or vendors on?
2. Do you write many congratulatory e-mails?
3. Have you received any congratulatory e-mails this year?

Sample Writing

Read the sample e-mail.

From: jasonseon@paragon.com
To: krichards@abcok.com
Subject: Congratulations on your success!

Hi Keith,

Congratulations on the success of your product launch! You and your team have done a wonderful job with Z100. The features are quite impressive. **I wish you continued success with this product.**

Sincerely,

Jason

발신: jasonseon@paragon.com
수신: krichards@abcok.com
제목: 성공을 축하드립니다!

안녕하세요, Keith.

제품 출시 성공을 축하드립니다! 당신과 당신 팀은 Z100을 아주 멋지게 만드셨습니다. 특징들이 꽤 인상적입니다. **이 제품의 지속적인 성공을 기원합니다.**

존경을 담아,

Jason

Comprehension Check

Answer the questions.

1. What is Jason congratulating Keith on?
2. What does Jason say is quite impressive?

Vocabulary

Match the words or expressions with the correct definitions.

1. success _____
2. product launch _____
3. feature _____
4. quite _____
5. impressive _____
6. wish _____

a. ~을 기원하다
b. 매우, 꽤
c. 제품 출시
d. 성공
e. 인상적인
f. 특징

✓ Vocab Test

Fill in the blanks with the correct words or expressions.

success / product launch / features / quite / impressive / wish

1. I might be _____ busy this week.
2. When is your _____?
3. Your presentation was _____.
4. That is the key to its continued _____.
5. It has many great _____.
6. I _____ you success.

⊕ Bonus Resources

hats off to someone 정말 잘하셨습니다, 경의를 표합니다

A: Congratulations on the new product launch. **Hats off to you** for doing such a wonderful job.
신제품 출시 축하드립니다. 그렇게 훌륭하게 일을 한 것에 대해 경의를 표합니다.

B: Thank you! 감사합니다!

예전에 누구에게 또는 특정 장소에서 경의를 표할 때 모자를 벗은 것에서 유래된 표현이다. 지금은 상대방이 무언가를 너무 잘했을 때 Hats off to you!라고 한다.

124

Grammar Points

Read the following and practice making sentences.

1. Congratulations on ~

> Congratulations on ~은 '~을 축하합니다'를 뜻한다. 뒤에는 성공을 축하하는 것을 명사로 붙인다. 이 표현은 격식 없는 상황뿐만 아니라 조금 더 격식을 차린 상황에서도 쓸 수 있다.
>
> Ex *Congratulations on your promotion.* 승진 축하드립니다.

a) Congratulations on _____. 수상을 축하드립니다.

b) Congratulations on _____. 당신의 성공을 축하드립니다.

c) Congratulations on moving to _____. 새 사무실로 이사하시게 된 것을 축하드립니다.

2. I wish you ~

> I wish you ~는 '당신에게 ~을 기원합니다'라는 패턴으로, 뒤에 상대방이 누릴 수 있기를 바라는 것을 붙인다. 아직 일어나지 않은 상황에서 소망이 담긴 표현이다.
>
> Ex *I wish you continued success.* 지속적인 성공을 기원합니다.

a) I wish you _____. 행운을 기원합니다.

b) I wish you _____ years of happiness. 더 많은 행복한 해들을 기원합니다.

c) I wish you a _____. 안전한 여행을 기원합니다.

Practice

Making Sentences

Practice writing sentences. Use the given words or use your own. Then, read your sentences to your partner or group.

1. You and your team have ~
   (done great work / made progress / worked hard)

   - _____
   - _____
   - _____

2. ~ be quite impressive
   (The design / The new features / The innovations)

   - _____
   - _____
   - _____

Editing Sentences

Find a mistake in the e-mail and correct it.

From: jimbean@abccorp.com
To: p.iger@goodstores.com
Subject: Congratulations on the New Store's Success

Hi Pam,

Congratulations ①<u>with</u> the success of the Gangnam store! You and your team ②<u>have done</u> an exceptional job. The store looks great. I ③<u>wish you</u> continued ④<u>success</u> with ⑤<u>the</u> brand.

Regards,

Jim

Real Writing

Write an e-mail based on the following scenarios. Exchange your e-mail with a partner and check your partner's e-mail for errors.

Scenario 1

> Write an e-mail to Evan, a client. Congratulate him on his promotion to director. Say he deserves it and that you wish him continued success in his career.

Scenario 2

> Write an e-mail to a vendor and congratulate the person on launching a new product. Wish the vendor success with the product.

From: casey.min@hpcparners.com
To: evanrohas@paragon.com
Subject: _____

_____
_____
_____

Homework

Write a short e-mail to congratulate someone.

_____
_____
_____

127

Warm Up Sample Answers
1. I can congratulate them on (their promotion / getting an award / finishing a project / their product launch).
2. (Yes, I / No, I don't) write many congratulatory e-mails.
3. Yes, I have. / No, I haven't.

Comprehension Check Answers
1. Jason is congratulating Keith on the success of his product launch.
2. Jason says the features are quite impressive.

Vocabulary Answers
1. d, 2. c, 3. f, 4. b, 5. e, 6. a

Vocab Test Answers
1. quite, 2. product launch, 3. impressive, 4. success, 5. features, 6. wish

Grammar Points Answers
1. a) (the/your) award b) your success c) (a/the) new office
2. a) good luck b) many more c) safe journey

Editing Sentences Answer
① with → on

Real Writing Sample Answer
Scenario 1
Subject: Congratulations on your promotion!

Hi Evan,

Congratulations on your promotion to director! You totally deserve it. I wish you continued success in your career.

Best regards,

Casey

Homework Sample Answer
Subject: Great job on the project!

Hi Anna,

Congratulations on the success of the project! Hats off to you for doing such a great job. I wish you continued success with other projects.

Regards,

Tom

Writing Tip

Occasions for Writing Congratulatory E-mails
축하 이메일을 쓰는 경우

① Promotion 승진

Congratulate people who get promoted. 승진하는 사람들을 축하한다.

 Congratulations on your promotion. 승진을 축하드립니다.

② New Position 새로운 직책

Congratulate if someone gets a new position or moves to a different company.
누군가 새로운 직책을 맡거나 회사를 옮기면 축하해 준다.

Congratulations on your new position as manager. 매니저로 새로운 직책에 임명되심을 축하드립니다.
Congratulations on your new position at ABC Corp. ABC 사에서의 새로운 직책을 축하드립니다.

③ Work Achievement 업무 성과

Congratulate people on achievements at work. 업무 성과를 축하해 준다.

Congratulations on the success of the project. 프로젝트 성공을 축하드립니다.
Congratulations on the opening of your new store. 신규 매장 개업을 축하드립니다.

④ Professional Achievement 커리어 성과

Also congratulate people on professional achievements. 커리어 성과 역시 축하해 준다.

Congratulations on receiving the Employee of the Year award. 올해의 직원상 수상을 축하드립니다.
Congratulations on being featured in Engineering Magazine.
〈Engineering 잡지〉에 나오신 것을 축하드립니다.

⑤ Personal Celebrations 개인 기념일

You can also congratulate people on their weddings, anniversaries, or children's graduations.
또한 결혼식이나 기념일, 자녀 졸업식 등을 축하할 수 있다.

Congratulations on your son's graduation. 아들의 졸업을 축하드립니다.
Congratulations on your wedding anniversary. 결혼기념일을 축하드립니다.

7 Giving Instructions

 Learning Objectives

- Learners can give step-by-step instructions to recipients.
- Learners can use expressions that describe the order of tasks.
- Learners can express the importance of certain activities.

 Warm Up

Work with a partner or in a group. Discuss the following questions.

1. How often do you give instructions via e-mail?
2. What is usually the subject matter?
3. Who do you usually provide instructions to?

Sample Writing

Read the sample e-mail.

From: billdoors@westsoft.com
To: stevewan@westsoft.com
Subject: RE: Problem with the Speaker

Hi Steve,

Here's what you can do to troubleshoot the problem. First, unplug the speaker. The red indicator light should go off. After that, plug the speaker back in. If the blue indicator light comes on, then the problem is solved. **Make sure to let me know what happens.**

Regards,

Bill

발신: billdoors@westsoft.com
수신: stevewan@westsoft.com
제목: RE: 스피커 문제

안녕하세요, Steve.

문제 해결을 위해 이렇게 하면 됩니다. 우선 스피커 플러그를 뽑으세요. 빨간 표시등이 꺼질 겁니다. 그런 다음, 스피커를 다시 꽂으세요. 파란 표시등이 켜지면 문제가 해결된 겁니다. 어떻게 되는지 저에게 꼭 알려줘요.

인사를 전하며,

Bill

✓ Comprehension Check

Answer the questions.

1. What should Steve do first?
2. What should Steve make sure to do?

Vocabulary

Match the words or expressions with the correct definitions.

1. troubleshoot _____
2. unplug _____
3. indicator light _____
4. go off _____
5. plug in _____
6. sure _____

a. (불, 전기 등이) 나가다
b. 표시등
c. 틀림없이, 확실히
d. (문제, 결함 등) 해결하다
e. 플러그를 뽑다
f. 플러그를 꽂는다

✓ Vocab Test

Fill in the blanks with the correct words or expressions.

troubleshoot / unplug / indicator light / go off / plug in / sure

1. I'm _____ it's true.
2. _____ the laptop.
3. _____ the TV and turn it on.
4. I need to _____ this problem.
5. If you unplug it, the light will _____.
6. Why is the _____ on?

⊕ Bonus Resources

take action 행동에 옮기다, 조치를 취하다

A: Make sure you do something about this. **Take action** right away.
이것에 대해 반드시 뭐라도 해야 합니다. 바로 조치를 취하세요.
B: I will. 그러겠습니다.

take action은 '액션을 취하다'라고 직역되며, 그 의미가 역동적으로 전달되는 표현이다.

Grammar Points

Read the following and practice making sentences.

1. Here's what ~

> Here's what ~은 '~이 이것이다'로 직역된다. 무언가를 지시하거나 사건을 서술, 목록을 제시할 때 아주 유용한 패턴이다.
>
> 📖 *Here's what you should do.* 이렇게 하셔야 합니다.

   a) Here's what you can _____. 이렇게 시도해 볼 수 있습니다.

   b) Here's what you should _____ first. 이렇게 먼저 하세요.

   c) Here's what I _____. 저는 이렇게 생각해요.

2. Make sure to ~

> Make sure to ~는 '반드시 ~을 하세요'라는 뜻으로, 뒤에 동사가 붙는다. 상대방이 꼭 취해야 할 행동을 단도직입적으로 지시할 때 쓴다. '~을 확실히 해 두세요'라는 의미로도 쓰인다.
>
> 📖 *Make sure to ask her.* 그녀에게 꼭 물어보세요.

   a) Make sure to _____ the door. 꼭 문을 닫으세요.

   b) Make sure to _____ Joe. 꼭 Joe에게 말해주세요.

   c) Make sure to _____ thank you. 꼭 고맙다고 말을 하세요.

Practice

Making Sentences

Practice writing sentences. Use the given words or use your own. Then, read your sentences to your partner or group.

1. First, ~

   (turn on the switch / push the button / open the package)

   - _____
   - _____
   - _____

2. After that, ~

   (clean the table / go home / call me)

   - _____
   - _____
   - _____

Editing Sentences

Find a mistake in the e-mail and correct it.

> From: pjsims@abccorp.com
> To: kharrington@abccorp.com
> Subject: RE: It's Not Working
>
> Hi Kit,
>
> Here's what ①<u>you can</u> try. ②<u>First</u>, open the cover. ③<u>After that</u>, see if there's any damage inside. ④<u>Make</u> sure ⑤<u>that</u> look carefully.
>
> Regards,
>
> P.J.

 **Real Writing**

Write an e-mail based on the following scenarios. Exchange your e-mail with a partner and check your partner's e-mail for errors.

Scenario 1

> Write an e-mail to Ronny, a coworker. Instruct him on what to do regarding a project binder. Tell him to first go to the third floor and pick it up from Dan. Then tell him to go all the way up to the fifth floor and give it to Susan. Add that he should make sure to give it to her in person.

Scenario 2

> Write a reply e-mail to a client. Give instructions on how to find your office from a subway stop.

From: wandavista@ktraining.com
To: ronnybest@ktraining.com
Subject: _____

_____
_____
_____

 **Homework**

Write a short e-mail to give instructions on how to solve a problem with the carpet.

_____
_____
_____

Warm Up Sample Answers
1. I give instructions via e-mail (often / very rarely / sometimes).
2. They are usually about (work processes / projects / technical matters).
3. I usually provide instructions to (coworkers/subordinates/vendors/suppliers/contractors).

Comprehension Check Answers
1. Steve should unplug the speaker first.
2. Steve should make sure to let Bill know what happens.

Vocabulary Answers
1. d, 2. e, 3. b, 4. a, 5. f, 6. c

Vocab Test Answers
1. sure, 2. Unplug, 3. Plug in, 4. troubleshoot, 5. go off, 6. indicator light

Grammar Points Answers
1. a) try b) do c) think
2. a) close b) tell c) say

Editing Sentences Answer
⑤ that → to

Real Writing Sample Answer
Scenario 1
Subject: Delivering the Project Binder

Hi Ronny,

Here's what you should do regarding the project binder. First, go to the third floor and pick it up from Dan. After that, go all the way up to the fifth floor and give the binder to Susan. Make sure to give it to her in person.

Regards,

Wanda

Homework Sample Answer
Subject: RE: Project Site Carpet Problem

Hi Tom,

Here's what you should do. First, go to the project site. After that, talk to the supervisor about the problem with the carpet. Make sure you ask him to take action today.

Regards,

Anna

Writing Tip

Questions to Ask Yourself Before Writing Instructions
자세한 설명을 쓰기 전에 스스로에게 할 질문

① What is the recipient trying to accomplish?
상대방이 완수하고자 하는 것이 무엇인가?

Be clear on exactly what the recipient needs to accomplish. The person might be trying to solve a problem. The person might also need step-by-step instructions.

수신자가 완수해야 하는 것이 무엇인지 명확하게 한다. 문제를 해결하려고 하는 걸 수 있다. 또한 단계별로 설명이 필요할 수도 있다.

② How much does the person know? 상대방의 해당 지식은 어느 정도인가?

Consider how much knowledge the person has about the subject matter. Then, you can think about how much information you will need to provide.

주제에 대해 수신자가 얼마나 많이 아는지를 고려한다. 그래야 얼마나 많은 정보를 제공해야 하는지 생각해 볼 수 있다.

③ What are the individual activities? 개별적인 업무가 무엇인가?

Think about what tasks or activities the person needs to complete.

수신자가 완수해야 할 업무들이 무엇인지 생각해 본다.

④ What are the exact steps? 정확한 단계들이 무엇인가?

Rearrange the tasks as needed. Use sequence adverbs to guide the recipient. Also, it's a good idea to explain what the result of each step should be.

필요시 단계를 재배열한다. 순서를 나타내는 부사를 사용해서 수신자의 이해를 돕는다. 각 단계의 결과가 무엇일지 설명하는 것도 좋은 생각이다.

> **Ex** *First* 우선
> *Next* 그다음에
> *Then* 그리곤
> *Finally* 마지막으로

8 Out-of-Office Message

 Learning Objectives

- Learners can write out-of-the-office messages.
- Learners can explain that they are going on vacation.
- Learners can give a contact name for emergencies.

 Warm Up

Work with a partner or in a group. Discuss the following questions.

1. Do you usually send out e-mails explaining you will be on vacation?
2. How long are your summer vacations?
3. Who usually takes care of your work while you are gone?

Sample Writing

Read the sample e-mail.

From: darrenk@westsoft.com
To: flynsey@abccorp.com
Subject: Going on Vacation

Hi Fiona,

I wanted to let you know my vacation plans. **I will be out of the office from Dec. 14 to Dec. 20.** I most likely won't be able to check e-mails. **If you need immediate assistance, please contact Anton Kim.** Thanks!

Best regards,

Darren

발신: darrenk@westsoft.com
수신: flynsey@abccorp.com
제목: 휴가 갑니다

안녕하세요, Fiona.

저의 휴가 계획을 알려드리고 싶었습니다. 저는 12월 14일부터 12월 20일까지 사무실 자리를 비웁니다. 아마 이메일 확인을 못 할 겁니다. 즉각적인 도움이 필요하시면 Anton Kim에게 연락해 주십시오. 감사합니다!

존경을 담아,

Darren

Comprehension Check

Answer the questions.

1. When will Darren be out of the office?
2. Who should Fiona contact for immediate assistance?

Vocabulary

Match the words or expressions with the correct definitions.

1. vacation plan _____
2. out of the office _____
3. most likely _____
4. able _____
5. immediate _____
6. assistance _____

a. 아마
b. 할 수 있는
c. 휴가 계획
d. 즉각적인
e. 도움
f. 사무실 자리를 비우는

✓ Vocab Test

Fill in the blanks with the correct words or expressions.

vacation plans / out of the office / most likely / able / immediate / assistance

1. I will be _____ to go tonight.
2. I need an _____ response.
3. I'll be _____ on Monday.
4. He _____ won't come.
5. Do you need any _____?
6. What are your _____?

⊕ Bonus Resources

on vacation/holiday 휴가 중

A: Where's Joe? I haven't seen him lately. Joe는 어디 계세요? 요즘 안 보여서요.
B: He's **on vacation**. 휴가 중입니다.

vacation(미국식)과 holiday(영국식)는 여름 등에 하는 '휴가'를 뜻하는데, on을 앞에 붙이면 '휴가 중'이 된다. 참고로 미국에서 holiday는 '공휴일', '휴일'을 뜻한다.

 **Grammar Points**

Read the following and practice making sentences.

1. I will be out of the office ~

> I will be out of the office ~를 직역하면 '사무실에서 나와 있겠다'가 되는데, '외부에 있겠다'는 뜻이다. 흔히 출장이나 휴가를 언급할 때 쓰는 표현이다.
>
> *I will be out of the office for a week.* 일주일 동안 사무실 자리를 비웁니다.

a) I will be out of the office all _____. 다음 주 내내 사무실 자리를 비웁니다.

b) I will be out of the office _____. 3일 동안 사무실 자리를 비웁니다.

c) I will be out of the office _____. 7월 1일부터 7월 5일까지 자리를 비웁니다.

2. If you need ~, please contact ~

> If you need A, please contact B는 'A가 필요하시면 B에게 연락해 주세요'라는 뜻이다. A는 필요한 것, B는 연락해야 할 사람이나 부서를 뜻한다.
>
> *If you need assistance, please contact Gary.* 도움이 필요하시면 Gary에게 연락해 주세요.

a) If you need _____, please contact me.

   무엇이든지 필요하시면 저에게 연락해 주세요.

b) If you need _____, please contact my office.

   사본이 필요하시면 제 사무실로 연락해 주세요.

c) If you need to place _____, please contact Penny.

   주문하시려면 Penny에게 연락해 주세요.

 **Practice**

Making Sentences

Practice writing sentences. Use the given words or use your own. Then, read your sentences to your partner or group.

1. I wanted to let you know ~

    (something / my contact number / the new date)

    - _____
    - _____
    - _____

2. I most likely ~

    (can't come / will see you tomorrow / will play golf)

    - _____
    - _____
    - _____

Editing Sentences

Find a mistake in the e-mail and correct it.

> From: pjsims@abccorp.com
> To: louislee@westsoft.com
> Subject: Not Available 04/19-22
>
> Hi Louis,
>
> I will be ①<u>out of</u> the office ②<u>in</u> April 19 to 22. ③<u>If you</u> need assistance, please ④<u>contact</u> J.K. ⑤<u>at</u> my office. Thanks!
>
> Regards,
>
> PJ

 Real Writing

Write an e-mail based on the following scenarios. Exchange your e-mail with a partner and check your partner's e-mail for errors.

Scenario 1

> Write an e-mail to JJ, a client. Say you'll be out of the office on September 2 and 4. Ask him to contact Pete Houser if he needs assistance.

Scenario 2

> Write an e-mail to a client and tell the person you'll be out of the office all next week. Provide the name of somebody the client can contact while you're away.

From: garywest@xyzcorp.com
To: jjnelson@abccorp.com
Subject: _____

_____
_____
_____

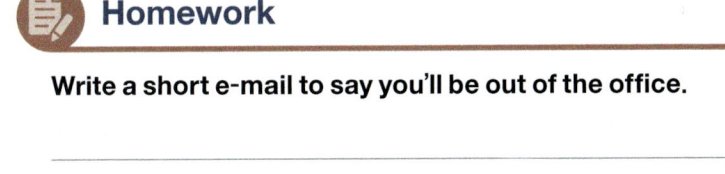 Homework

Write a short e-mail to say you'll be out of the office.

_____
_____
_____

Warm Up Sample Answers
1. (Yes, I / No, I don't) usually send out e-mails explaining I'll be on vacation.
2. My summer vacations are usually (a week / only a few days / five days) long. / It depends.
3. (A coworker / My boss / Someone on my team) usually takes care of my work while I'm gone.

Comprehension Check Answers
1. Darren will be out of the office from Dec. 14 to Dec. 20.
2. She should contact Anton Kim.

Vocabulary Answers
1. c, 2. f, 3. a, 4. b, 5. d, 6. e

Vocab Test Answers
1. able, 2. immediate, 3. out of the office, 4. most likely, 5. assistance, 6. vacation plans

Grammar Points Answers
1. a) next week b) for three days c) from July 1 to July 5
2. a) anything b) a copy c) an order

Editing Sentences Answer
② in → from

Real Writing Sample Answer
Scenario 1
Subject: Out of the Office 09/02 & 09/04

Hi JJ,

I will be out of the office on September 2 and 4. If you need assistance, please contact Pete Houser. Thanks!

Regards,

Gary

Homework Sample Answer
Subject: On Vacation Next Week

Hi Anna,

I will be out of the office on vacation all next week. I won't be able to answer my e-mails. If you need immediate assistance, please contact Anne or Terry.

Regards,

Tom

Writing Tip

Extra Expressions to Use for Out-of-Office E-mails
부재 알림 이메일에 쓸 수 있는 추가 표현

① E-mail Access 이메일 접속

EX *I won't be able to access my e-mail.* 제 이메일을 접속할 수 없을 겁니다.
Access to my e-mail will be limited. 이메일 접속이 제한될 겁니다.

② Return to Office 사무실 복귀

EX *I'll be back at the office on January 15.* 1월 15일에 사무실로 복귀합니다.
I'm returning to the office on January 15. 1월 15일에 사무실로 복귀합니다.

③ Send an E-mail 이메일 보내기

EX *If you need to reach me, send me an e-mail.* 저에게 연락하시려면 저에게 이메일을 보내주세요.
I'll be checking my e-mail regularly. 제 이메일을 정기적으로 확인할 겁니다.

④ Leave a Message 메시지 남기기

EX *You can leave a message with Cecil Hendricks.* Cecil Hendricks에게 메시지를 남기시면 됩니다.
Please leave a message with Cecil Hendricks. Cecil Hendricks에게 메시지를 남겨주세요.

⑤ Answering 답변하기

EX *I'll try to get back to you as soon as I can.* 가능한 한 빨리 답변을 드리겠습니다.
I'll try and answer as soon as I can. 가능한 한 빨리 답변을 드리겠습니다.

⑥ Expressions Indicating Specific Periods 일정 기간에 대한 표현

EX *for a few days* 며칠 동안
the whole week/month 일주일 / 한 달 내내
all day/week 하루 종일 / 일주일 내내
from Monday to Wednesday 월요일부터 수요일까지

9 Making Announcements

 Learning Objectives

- Learners can make announcements via e-mail.
- Learners can send out official notices.
- Learners can recommend or request action based on the announcement.

 Warm Up

Work with a partner or in a group. Discuss the following questions.

1. How often do you have to make announcements via e-mail?
2. What are your announcements usually about?
3. Do you get announcements via e-mail often?

Sample Writing

Read the sample e-mail.

From: rforeman@paragon.com
To: All
Subject: Temp Office Closure

Hello everyone,

I'm writing to inform you that our office building will be closed due to maintenance. It will last from October 2 to October 6. **We ask that you work from home during this period.** For any questions, please contact me.

Regards,

Ron Foreman

발신: rforeman@paragon.com
수신: 전 직원
제목: 임시 사무실 폐쇄

모두 안녕하세요.

보수로 인해 우리 사무실 빌딩이 문을 닫는다고 알리기 위해 이메일 드립니다. 10월 2일부터 10월 6일까지 이어집니다. 이 기간에 재택근무를 해주시기를 바랍니다. 질문이 있으면 저에게 연락해 주세요.

수고하세요.

Ron Foreman

Comprehension Check

Answer the questions.

1. Why is the building being closed?
2. What is Ron asking everyone to do during this period?

Vocabulary

Match the words or expressions with the correct definitions.

1. write to _____
2. inform _____
3. due to _____
4. maintenance _____
5. last _____
6. work from home _____

a. ~을 위해 (이메일을) 쓰다
b. 보수
c. (특정한 시간 동안) 계속되다
d. 재택근무하다
e. ~으로 인하여, ~ 때문에
f. 알리다

✓ Vocab Test

Fill in the blanks with the correct words or expressions.

writing to / informed / due to / maintenance / last / work from home

1. Our office will be closed for _____.
2. The problem is _____ delivery.
3. Nowadays, many people _____.
4. He _____ everyone.
5. The meeting will _____ one hour.
6. I'm _____ answer your question.

⊕ Bonus Resources

take (something) into consideration ~을 고려하다

A: Make sure you **take** the budget **into consideration**.
예산을 꼭 고려해 주세요.
B: Of course. 물론이죠.

consider와 비슷하지만 take ~ into consideration은 '확실히 고려하다'라는 뉘앙스가 강하다.

 **Grammar Points**

Read the following and practice making sentences.

1. I'm writing to inform you that ~

> I'm writing은 글을 쓴다는 뜻인데, 이메일에서는 '이메일을 쓴다'를 의미한다. 이에 따라 I'm writing to inform you that ~은 '~을 알리기 위해 이메일 드립니다'가 된다. 공식적 공지를 보낼 때 주로 쓴다.
>
> *I'm writing to inform you that I will be out of the office next week.*
> 제가 다음 주 사무실 자리를 비운다는 걸 알리기 위해 이메일 드립니다.

a) I'm writing to inform you that I'm going _____.
휴가 간다는 걸 알리기 위해 이메일 드립니다.

b) I'm writing to inform you that there will be _____ tomorrow.
내일 회의가 없다는 걸 알리기 위해 이메일 드립니다.

c) I'm writing to inform you that we will be _____ next Monday.
다음 주 월요일 휴무라는 걸 알리기 위해 이메일 드립니다.

2. We ask that you ~

> 직역으로는 '당신이 ~하라고 묻다'지만 실은 '당신에게 ~을 바란다'라는 뜻이다. 상대방에게 요청하는 행동을 동사원형으로 뒤에 붙인다.
>
> *We ask that you remain seated.* 계속 앉아 계시기를 바랍니다.

a) We ask that you _____. 함께 일하시기를 바랍니다.

b) We ask that you _____. 저희에게 전화 주시기를 바랍니다.

c) We ask that you _____. John과 얘기하시기를 바랍니다.

Practice

Making Sentences

Practice writing sentences. Use the given words or use your own. Then, read your sentences to your partner or group.

1. It will last ~

    (from Monday to Friday / 3 days / a long time)

    - _____
    - _____
    - _____

2. For any questions, ~

    (call me / talk to your supervisor / please email me)

    - _____
    - _____
    - _____

Editing Sentences

Find a mistake in the e-mail and correct it.

> From: dsanders@paragon.com
> To: All
> Subject: Potluck Party on Dec. 20
>
> Hello everyone,
>
> ①I'm writing ②to inform you that there will be a potluck party on December 20 at 4 P.M. It ③will be held in the first-floor lobby. We ④say that you bring a dish or some soda. ⑤For any questions, call me!
>
> Regards,
>
> Diane

Real Writing

Write an e-mail based on the following scenarios. Exchange your e-mail with a partner and check your partner's e-mail for errors.

Scenario 1

> Write an e-mail to Jim, a delivery truck driver. Tell him loading dock 2 is closed due to maintenance. It will reopen this Friday. Ask him to use either dock 1 or dock 3.

Scenario 2

> Write an e-mail to all the employees. Say that the company will be closed due to the Chuseok holidays. Ask them to send out announcements to their contacts to tell them this.

From: melipson@fastlog.com
To: jimseam@fastlog.com
Subject: _____

_____
_____
_____

Homework

Write a short e-mail announcing that your office will be closed.

_____
_____
_____

Warm Up Sample Answers
1. I make announcements via e-mail (maybe once a month / quite often). / I rarely make announcements via e-mail.
2. My announcements are usually about (schedules/projects/reports/tasks/meetings).
3. (Yes, I / No, I don't) get announcements via e-mail often.

Comprehension Check Answers
1. It is being closed for maintenance.
2. He is asking them to work from home.

Vocabulary Answers
1. a, 2. f, 3. e, 4. b, 5. c, 6. d

Vocab Test Answers
1. maintenance, 2. due to, 3. work from home, 4. informed, 5. last, 6. writing to

Grammar Points Answers
1. a) on vacation b) no meeting c) closed
2. a) work together b) call us c) talk to John

Editing Sentences Answer
④ say that → ask that

Real Writing Sample Answer
Scenario 1
Subject: Loading Dock 2 Temporarily Closed

Hi Jim,

I'm writing to inform you that loading dock 2 is closed due to maintenance. It will reopen this Friday. Meanwhile, we ask that you use either dock 1 or dock 3. For any question, please contact me.

Regards,

Mel

Homework Sample Answer
Subject: Office Closed Until Friday

Hi Ella,

I'm writing to inform you that our office building will be closed for repair work due to water damage. It will last from tomorrow to Friday. We ask that you take this into consideration when making plans to visit us. For any questions, please contact me.

Regards,

Adam

Writing Tip

Writing Negative News with the Direct Approach
단도직입적인 방식으로 부정적인 소식 쓰기

It's a good idea to be indirect when giving really bad news. However, if the news is about something temporary, routine, or urgent, you should be direct.
아주 나쁜 소식을 전할 때는 우회적인 어조를 쓰는 것이 좋다. 하지만 해당 소식이 임시적이거나 일반적이거나, 긴급하다면 단도직입적인 접근이 요구된다.

① Begin with the bad news. 나쁜 소식으로 시작한다.

At the beginning of the e-mail, be direct with the negative news. Avoid slang and language that is too casual.
이메일 도입부에 부정적인 소식을 단도직입적으로 언급한다. 속어나 과도하게 격식 없는 표현은 삼간다.

Ex *Unfortunately, we won't be able to accept your proposal.* 안타깝지만, 귀사의 제안서를 수락할 수 없습니다.

② Give additional info. 추가 정보를 준다.

If necessary, give the reason or background for the negative news. Also, add any details that may help the recipient. Be careful even if you think you need to apologize. Remember that an apology might be used to justify a claim against you.
필요하다면 부정적인 소식과 연관된 이유나 배경을 설명한다. 수신자에게 도움이 될 만한 세부 사항도 추가한다. 사과가 필요하다는 생각이 드는 경우에도 주의가 필요하다. 사과가 클레임으로 이어질 수 있다는 점을 염두에 둔다.

Ex *The prices you indicated are too high.* 표시하신 가격들이 너무 높습니다.

③ End in a courteous way. 공손하게 마무리한다.

Say something positive if possible. Be courteous. You can add expressions such as "Thank you for your understanding" if needed. You can tell the recipient to contact you or your team if he or she has any questions.
가능하다면 무언가 긍정적인 것을 언급한다. 예의를 지킨다. 필요하다면 '이해해 주셔서 감사합니다'와 같은 표현을 추가할 수 있다. 수신자에게 궁금한 점이 있으면 본인이나 본팀에 연락하라고 말해도 좋다.

Ex *We thank you for taking the time to send us the proposal.* 시간을 내서 제안서를 보내주셔서 감사드립니다.

10 Sharing Good News

 Learning Objectives

- Learners can share good news via e-mail.
- Learners can provide details about the good news.
- Learners can use appropriately positive expressions for the good news.

 Warm Up

Work with a partner or in a group. Discuss the following questions.

1. How often do you write e-mails with good news?
2. Who do you usually write e-mails with good news to?
3. What is the most difficult thing about writing this type of e-mail?

Sample Writing

Read the sample e-mail.

> From: vivianlee@xyzcorp.com
> To: bjohnson@paragon.com
> Subject: We sold one million units!
>
> Hi Ben,
>
> **I'd like to share some great news with you. XYZ Corp. is thrilled to announce our millionth unit sold.** We want to thank you for helping to make this happen. This wouldn't have been possible without your support.
>
> Best regards,
>
> Vivian

발신: vivianlee@xyzcorp.com
수신: bjohnson@paragon.com
제목: 100만 대가 나갔어요!

안녕하세요, Ben.

아주 좋은 소식을 공유하고 싶습니다. XYZ 사는 저희의 백만 대 판매량 달성을 알리게 되어 매우 기쁘게 생각합니다. 이를 실현하는 데 도움을 주셔서 감사드리고 싶습니다. 귀하의 지원 없이는 가능하지 않았을 겁니다.

존경을 담아,

Vivian

Comprehension Check

Answer the questions.

1. What is the great news?
2. Who does Vivian want to thank for helping to make this happen?

Vocabulary

Match the words or expressions with the correct definitions.

1. share _____	a. 매우 기쁜
2. thrilled _____	b. ~를 실현하다
3. unit _____	c. 지원
4. help to _____	d. ~하기를 돕다
5. make ~ happen _____	e. 공유하다
6. support _____	f. 제품 (1대)

✓ Vocab Test

Fill in the blanks with the correct words or expressions.

shared / thrilled / units / helping to / make this happen / support

1. How many _____ were sold?
2. I _____ the news with the team.
3. Let's _____.
4. I'm _____ that you're coming.
5. Thank you for your _____.
6. He's _____ solve the problem.

⊕ Bonus Resources

reach a milestone 중대한 단계 / 주요 지점에 도달하다

A: We just sold our thousandth unit. 막 천 대 판매량을 달성했습니다.
B: Wow! You've **reached a milestone**. 와! 중대한 단계에 도달했네요.

milestone은 이정표를 의미하는데, 비즈니스 상황에서 언급될 때는 어떤 중요한 단계나 주요 지점을 뜻한다. 프로젝트 일정 자체에도 표시하는 경우가 많다.

Grammar Points

Read the following and practice making sentences.

1. I'd like to share some great news ~

> 다소 길게 느껴질 수도 있는 I'd like to share some great news ~는 '아주 좋은 소식을 공유하고 싶다'를 뜻한다. 좋은 소식을 알릴 때 유익한 표현으로 뒤에는 주로 전치사(about/with/regarding 등)가 붙는다.
>
> *I'd like to share some great news* about the promotion. 승진에 대한 아주 좋은 소식을 공유하고 싶습니다.

a) I'd like to share some great news about _____.
   팀에 대한 아주 좋은 소식을 공유하고 싶습니다.

b) I'd like to share some great news with _____.
   모두와 아주 좋은 소식을 공유하고 싶습니다.

c) I'd like to share some great news regarding _____.
   프로젝트에 대한 아주 좋은 소식을 공유하고 싶습니다.

2. ~ be thrilled to announce ~

> be thrilled to announce ~는 '~을 알리게 되어 매우 기쁩니다'를 뜻한다. 뒤에는 다양한 품사가 따르는데, 명사가 오는 경우도 있고, that 절이 붙기도 한다.
>
> We *are thrilled to announce* the opening of our new store.
> 저희 새 매장의 개장을 알리게 되어 매우 기쁘게 생각합니다.

a) I am thrilled to announce _____ John Lee as the new CEO.
   John Lee가 새로운 CEO로 임명된 것을 알리게 되어 매우 기쁘게 생각합니다.

b) Ace Books is thrilled to announce that *Go Anthology* _____ the bestseller list.
   Ace Books는 〈Go Anthology〉가 베스트셀러 목록에 올랐다는 걸 알리게 되어 매우 기쁘게 생각합니다.

c) We are thrilled to announce that _____ a branch office in Busan.
   당사가 부산에 지사를 연 것을 알리게 되어 매우 기쁘게 생각합니다.

 **Practice**

Making Sentences

Practice writing sentences. Use the given words or use your own. Then, read your sentences to your partner or group.

1. We want to thank you for ~

   (the gift / your support / understanding)

   - _____
   - _____
   - _____

2. This wouldn't have been possible without ~

   (your contribution / your staff / everyone's hard work)

   - _____
   - _____
   - _____

Editing Sentences

Find a mistake in the e-mail and correct it.

> From: vichunter@gogames.com
> To: jbridge@paragon.com
> Subject: Reached 100K downloads!
>
> Hi Jeff,
>
> I'd like to share ①<u>some</u> great news ②<u>for</u> you. We are thrilled to ③<u>announce</u> that the new game has reached 100,000 downloads. We ④<u>want to</u> thank you for your team's ⑤<u>ongoing</u> support.
>
> Regards,
>
> Victor

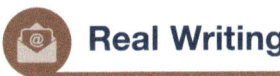

Real Writing

Write an e-mail based on the following scenarios. Exchange your e-mail with a partner and check your partner's e-mail for errors.

Scenario 1

> Write an e-mail to Austin, a designer. Announce that your company KC Inc. has just won the World Innovation Award. Thank him for his valuable contribution to the design.

Scenario 2

> Write an e-mail to a client. Announce that your company has just released a new line of sweaters.

From: jlanders@kcinc.com
To: austin.lee@kdesign.com
Subject: _____

_____
_____
_____

Homework

Write a short e-mail to share some great news about your website.

_____
_____
_____

Warm Up Sample Answers
1. I write e-mails with good news (often / once a month / sometimes / only rarely).
2. I usually write e-mails with good news to (coworkers / clients / shareholders / the public).
3. It's difficult to (find the right expressions / sound enthusiastic).

Comprehension Check Answers
1. XYZ Corp. has sold one million units.
2. She wants to thank Ben.

Vocabulary Answers
1. e, 2. a, 3. f, 4. d, 5. b, 6. c

Vocab Test Answers
1. units, 2. shared, 3. make this happen, 4. thrilled, 5. support, 6. helping to

Grammar Points Answers
1. a) the team b) everyone c) the project
2. a) the appointment of b) has reached c) we have opened

Editing Sentences Answer
② for → with

Real Writing Sample Answer
Scenario 1
Subject: We won the World Innovation Award!

Dear Austin,

I'd like to share some great news. KC Inc. is thrilled to announce that it has just won the World Innovation Award. We want to thank you for your valuable contribution to the design.

Regards,

Jack Landers

Homework Sample Answer
Subject: 1 Million Hits in November

Hi Mona,

I'd like to share some great news. We are thrilled to announce that our website got 1 million hits last month. We want to thank you for helping us reach this milestone.

Regards,

Ian

Writing Tip

Types of Good News to Share
공유할 만한 좋은 소식의 종류

① Launching new products or services 새 제품이나 서비스를 출시할 때

You might be rolling out a new product or introducing a new service to the market.
신규 제품을 출시하거나, 새로운 서비스를 시장에 내놓는 중일 수도 있다.

> **Ex** We are excited to announce the launch of our new website.
> 당사의 신규 웹사이트 개설을 알리게 되어 매우 기쁘게 생각합니다.

② Opening new stores or facilities 새 매장이나 시설을 열 때

You might be opening a new store or office. 새 매장이나 새 사무실을 여는 중일 수도 있다.

> **Ex** We are excited to announce the opening of our Gangnam store.
> 저희 강남 매장 개장을 알리게 되어 매우 기쁘게 생각합니다.

③ Appointing new executives 신규 임원을 임명할 때

Hiring or promoting important executives is a good occasion to send out an e-mail.
중요한 임원의 채용이나 승진은 이메일을 내보낼 만한 좋은 경우이다.

> **Ex** We are excited to announce the appointment of Ms. Cindy Lopez as our new director of sales.
> Ms. Cindy Lopez가 새로운 영업이사로 임명됨을 알리게 되어 매우 기쁘게 생각합니다.

④ Engaging in community activities 지역 사회 활동에 참여할 때

Every company needs to contribute to society. When you do something good for the community, let people know.
어떤 기업이든 사회에 기여해야 한다. 지역 사회에서 좋은 일을 할 때는 이를 알린다.

> **Ex** We are excited to announce that we're taking part in the annual fundraiser for the Seoul Shelter for the Homeless.
> 서울 노숙자 쉼터를 위한 연례 모금 행사에 참여함을 알리게 되어 매우 기쁘게 생각합니다.

11 Writing Invitations

 Learning Objectives

- Learners can invite people to events.
- Learners can provide instructions on how to RSVP.
- Learners can provide additional information about the event.

 Warm Up

Work with a partner or in a group. Discuss the following questions.

1. Have you ever invited people to events via e-mail?
2. What was the most recent company event you were part of?
3. What types of guests did you invite to the most recent event?

Sample Writing

Read the sample e-mail.

From: jpark@paragon.com
To: jeffbean@xyzcorp.com
Subject: Invitation to Annual Soft Insight Conference

Dear Mr. Bean,

We are delighted to invite you to our annual Soft Insight Conference. It will be held on December 5 at 7 P.M., at the Hotel Seoul. **To secure your spot at this exclusive event, kindly RSVP by November 30.** We hope to see you there!

Best regards,

Janice Park

발신: jpark@paragon.com
수신: jeffbean@xyzcorp.com
제목: 연례 Soft Insight 콘퍼런스 초대

안녕하세요, Bean님.

당사의 연례 Soft Insight 콘퍼런스에 귀하를 초대하게 되어 기쁩니다. 12월 5일 저녁 7시에 Hotel Seoul에서 진행될 것입니다. 이 특별 행사에 자리를 확보하시려면, 11월 30일까지 참석 여부를 알려주시기를 바랍니다. 거기서 뵙기를 기대합니다!

존경을 담아,

Janice Park

Comprehension Check

Answer the questions.

1. Where will the event be held?
2. When is the last day to RSVP?

Vocabulary

Match the words or expressions with the correct definitions.

1. delighted _____
2. be held on _____
3. secure _____
4. spot _____
5. kindly _____
6. RSVP _____

a. 부디 (정중하게 부탁할 때 쓰는 표현)
b. 기쁜
c. 자리
d. ~에 진행되다, ~에 열리다
e. 확보하다
f. 참석 여부 회신 바람

⊘ Vocab Test

Fill in the blanks with the correct words or expressions.

delighted / be held on / secured / spot / kindly / RSVP

1. The meeting will _____ Monday.
2. _____ send us a proposal.
3. I'd be _____ if you could come.
4. I _____ a seat.
5. Is there a _____ for me?
6. Please _____ by May 2.

⊕ Bonus Resources

host an event 행사를 주최하다

A: We're **hosting the event** this year. 올해는 저희가 행사를 주최합니다.
B: Really? You must be busy. 정말요? 많이 바쁘시겠어요.

여기서 host는 동사로 '주최하다'며, host an event는 '행사를 주최한다'는 뜻이다. 명사로 host라고 할 때는 '주최 측', '주인'이라는 뜻이다. 흔히 공식 회사 행사나 규모가 있는 행사 때 host라는 단어를 쓴다.

 **Grammar Points**

Read the following and practice making sentences.

1. We are delighted to invite you to ~

> We are delighted to invite you to ~는 상대방을 행사나 회의 등에 초대할 때 쓰기에 유용한 패턴이다. 비교적 격식을 차린 이메일이나 비즈니스 레터, 초대장에서 자주 쓴다.
>
> 📧 *We are delighted to invite you to* our grand opening. 저희 개업식에 귀하를 초대하게 되어 기쁩니다.

  a) We are delighted to invite you to a _____.
      VIP 세일에 귀하를 초대하게 되어 기쁩니다.

  b) We are delighted to invite you to a _____.
      특별 전시회에 귀하를 초대하게 되어 기쁩니다.

  c) We are delighted to invite you to our _____.
      당사 연례 파티에 귀하를 초대하게 되어 기쁩니다.

2. To secure a spot ~

> To secure a spot ~은 '~자리 확보를 위해'를 뜻한다. 흔히 뒤에는 '~에'를 의미하는 at이 붙는다.
>
> 📧 *To secure a spot* at the concert, please call me. 콘서트 자리를 확보하시려면, 저에게 전화 주세요.

  a) To secure a spot at this event, please _____.
      이 행사에 자리를 확보하시려면, 참석 여부를 알려주시기를 바랍니다.

  b) To secure a spot at the seminar, please _____.
      세미나에 자리를 확보하시려면, 전화 주시기를 바랍니다.

  c) To secure a spot at this special event, you can _____.
      이 특별 행사에 자리를 확보하시려면, 저에게 문자를 주셔도 됩니다.

 **Practice**

Making Sentences

Practice writing sentences. Use the given words or use your own. Then, read your sentences to your partner or group.

1. It will be held ~

   (on March 20 / at our office / in the conference room)

   -
   -
   -

2. We hope to see you ~

   (there / at the party / on Friday)

   -
   -
   -

Editing Sentences

Find a mistake in the e-mail and correct it.

From: pjennings@paragon.com
To: vicgaines@gogames.com
Subject: Invitation to End-of-the-Year Party

Dear Vic,

We are delighted to ①<u>invitation</u> you to our annual end-of-the-year party. It will be held on December 20 at 8 P.M. ②<u>in</u> our lobby. To ③<u>secure</u> your spot, please send me a reply e-mail ④<u>by</u> December 15. ⑤<u>See</u> you there!

Regards,

Paul Jennings

 ## Real Writing

Write an e-mail based on the following scenarios. Exchange your e-mail with a partner and check your partner's e-mail for errors.

Scenario 1

> Write an e-mail to Andy, a vendor's rep. Invite him to the grand opening of your Jongno store on March 15 at 3 P.M. To secure his spot, tell him he can simply let you know by March 5.

Scenario 2

> Write an e-mail to a client and invite the person to your annual customer appreciation party on December 1 at 7 P.M. at your office. The client should RSVP by November 25.

From: barrykim@sstores.com
To: a.wayne@abccorp.com
Subject: _____

_____
_____
_____

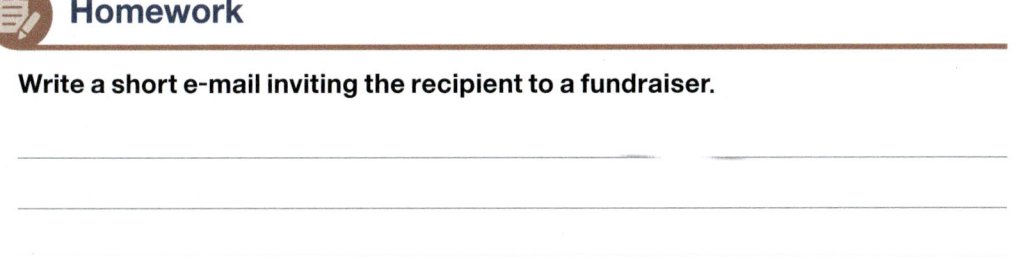 ## Homework

Write a short e-mail inviting the recipient to a fundraiser.

_____
_____
_____

Warm Up Sample Answers
1. (Yes, I have / No, I have never) invited people to events via e-mail.
2. I was part of (a company party / a product launch / a company-sponsored seminar).
3. I invited (clients / customers / potential customers / vendors / subcontractors / members of the general public).

Comprehension Check Answers
1. It will be held at the Hotel Seoul.
2. The last day to RSVP is November 30.

Vocabulary Answers
1. b, 2. d, 3. e, 4. c, 5. a, 6. f

Vocab Test Answers
1. be held on, 2. Kindly, 3. delighted, 4. secured, 5. spot, 6. RSVP

Grammar Points Answers
1. a) VIP sale b) special exhibit c) annual party
2. a) RSVP b) call me c) text me

Editing Sentences Answer
① invitation → invite

Real Writing Sample Answer
Scenario 1
Subject: Jongno Grand Opening

Dear Andy,

We are delighted to invite you to the grand opening of our Jongno store. It will be held on March 15 at 3 P.M. To secure your spot, simply let me know by March 5. Hope to see you there.

Best regards,

Barry

Homework Sample Answer
Subject: We're Hosting the Share Fundraiser

Hi Vera,

We are delighted to invite you to the Share Fundraiser at the Milton Hotel. We are hosting the event this year. It will be held on December 27 at 4 P.M. To secure your spot, kindly RSVP by December 22. We hope you can make it.

Regards,

Eun Kim

Writing Tip

Formal Invitation Format
정식 초대장 양식

For more formal events, it might be a good idea to send out formal invitations. You can send the invitations via mail or as e-mail attachments. Here's a classic format.
다소 격식을 차린 공식 행사는 정식 초대장을 보내는 것도 좋은 방법이다. 우편이나 이메일 첨부파일로 초대장을 보낼 수 있다. 아래에 전통 양식 하나를 소개한다.

Paragon Korea Inc. cordially invites you to its Annual Holidays Dinner on Thursday, the twenty-first of December from five to nine o'clock. Ballroom A The Hotel Seoul Seoul, Korea RSVP 000-0000-0000 Formal Dress	Paragon Korea 사는 12월 21일 목요일 5시부터 9시까지 하는 연례 연휴 만찬에 귀하를 정중히 초대합니다. 연회장 A The Hotel Seoul 대한민국, 서울시 참석 여부 답변 요망 000-0000-0000 정장 차림

The invitation is usually printed on a card. As with most formal invitations, the words are aligned in the center.
보통 초대장은 카드에 인쇄된다. 대부분의 정식 초대장이 그렇듯이, 글자는 가운데에 맞추어진다.

"RSVP" is written at the bottom. A contact number is also included. If there is a dress code, that information is also placed at the bottom.
'참석 여부 답변 요망'은 하단에 명시된다. 연락처도 포함된다. 복장 규정이 있다면 그 정보 또한 하단에 표시된다.

12 Holiday Greetings

Learning Objectives

- Learners can send holiday greetings via e-mail.
- Learners can express appreciation or gratitude.
- Learners can express their hopes of continuing the relationship with the recipient.

Warm Up

Work with a partner or in a group. Discuss the following questions.
1. Have you ever sent holiday greetings via e-mail?
2. Who did you send the holiday greetings to?
3. What countries do many of your business contacts live in?

Sample Writing

Read the sample e-mail.

From: kenpark@paragon.com
To: nmchenry@xyzcorp.com
Subject: Happy Holidays from Paragon!

Hi Nat,

Happy holidays! **We wanted to send you our warmest greetings and best wishes for the holiday season. You've been an amazing business partner.** It's been a great year! We are excited about continuing to work with you next year.

Best regards,

Ken

발신: kenpark@paragon.com
수신: nmchenry@xyzcorp.com
제목: Paragon에서 겨울 명절 인사 보냅니다!

안녕하세요, Nat.

연휴 행복하게 보내세요! **연휴 시즌에 따뜻한 인사와 함께 행복을 기원하고 싶습니다. 당신은 멋진 비즈니스 협력자가 돼 주셨습니다.** 멋진 한해였습니다! 내년에도 함께 일할 것이 기대됩니다.

존경을 담아,

Ken

Comprehension Check

Answer the questions.

1. What is Ken thanking Nat for?
2. What is Ken looking forward to next year?

Vocabulary

Match the words or expressions with the correct definitions.

1. warmest greetings _____
2. best wishes _____
3. holiday season _____
4. amazing _____
5. business partner _____
6. continue to _____

a. 연휴 시즌
b. 멋진, 대단한
c. (연휴 시즌에 하는) 따뜻한 인사
d. (행복 또는 성공에 대한) 기원
e. ~을 계속하다
f. 비즈니스 협력자, 협력업체

✓ Vocab Test

Fill in the blanks with the correct words or expressions.

warmest greetings / best wishes / holiday season / amazing / business partner / continue to

1. _____ to you and your family!
2. You are _____!
3. Tom Carpenter is our _____.
4. We send you our _____.
5. We will _____ work with you.
6. Have a great _____.

⊕ Bonus Resources

(get into) the holiday spirit 겨울 명절 분위기(에 잠기다)

A: Let's have a Christmas party. 우리 크리스마스 파티합시다.
B: Yes! Let's **get into the holiday spirit**! 그래요! 겨울 명절 분위기를 만끽하자고요!

여기서 holiday는 미국 크리스마스와 연말을 합한 겨울 명절 기간, spirit은 '기분, 분위기'를 뜻한다. 흔히 한해 힘들었던 일들을 잊고 명절을 맞아 기분 좋고 여유 있게 행동하자고 친한 사람들끼리 얘기할 때 쓴다.

Grammar Points

Read the following and practice making sentences.

1. We wanted to send you our warmest greetings and best wishes ~

> We wanted to send you our warmest greetings and best wishes ~는 겨울 축제 기간에 쓰는 인사말이다. 실은 our warmest greetings와 best wishes 중 한 표현만 써도 좋다. 여기서 wanted는 '~을 하고 싶었다'지만 사실상 현재를 뜻하는 '~하고 싶다'로 번역된다.
>
> ▣ *We wanted to send you our warmest greetings and best wishes* for a joyous Christmas.
> 즐거운 크리스마스에 따뜻한 인사와 함께 행복을 기원하고 싶습니다.

a) We wanted to send you our warmest greetings and best wishes this _____.
이번 크리스마스 시즌에 따뜻한 인사와 함께 행복을 기원하고 싶습니다.

b) We wanted to send you our warmest greetings and best wishes for _____.
다가오는 해에 따뜻한 인사와 함께 행복을 기원하고 싶습니다.

c) We wanted to send you our warmest greetings and best wishes during _____.
겨울 명절 기간에 따뜻한 인사와 함께 행복을 기원하고 싶습니다.

2. You've been ~

> You've been ~은 '당신은 ~돼 주셨습니다'라는 뜻이다. 뒤에는 an amazing, a fantastic, a great 등 긍정적인 느낌이 담긴 형용사와 함께 직책이나 역할을 붙인다.
>
> ▣ *You've been a great host.* 멋진 주최자가 돼 주셨습니다.

a) You've been a wonderful _____. 멋진 고객이 돼 주셨습니다.

b) You've been a fantastic _____. 멋진 매니저가 돼 주셨습니다.

c) You've been an amazing _____. 멋진 회계사가 돼 주셨습니다.

 **Practice**

Making Sentences

Practice writing sentences. Use the given words or use your own. Then, read your sentences to your partner or group.

1. It's been a ~

   (great day / long time / pleasure talking to you)

   •
   •
   •

2. We are excited about ~

   (meeting you / talking to you / working with you)

   •
   •
   •

Editing Sentences

Find a mistake in the e-mail and correct it.

From: jeanhan@paragon.com
To: wsnyder@xyzcorp.com
Subject: Happy holidays!

Hi Warren,

We wanted to ①<u>say</u> you our warmest greetings and ②<u>best</u> wishes for the holidays. You've ③<u>been</u> a great business partner. ④<u>We</u> look forward to ⑤<u>working with</u> you again next year.

Regards,

Jean

Real Writing

Write an e-mail based on the following scenarios. Exchange your e-mail with a partner and check your partner's e-mail for errors.

Scenario 1

> Write an e-mail to Dean, a client. Say you're sending your warmest greetings and best wishes. Thank him for being a wonderful client. Add that you look forward to working with him for many more years.

Scenario 2

> Write an e-mail to a vendor and send your best wishes for the holidays. Thank the vendor for being a great business partner.

From: barrymason@paragon.com
To: dkim@abccorp.com
Subject: _____

_____

_____

_____

Homework

Write a short holiday greetings e-mail.

_____

_____

_____

Warm Up Sample Answers
1. (Yes, I have / No, I have never) sent holiday greetings via e-mail.
2. I sent greetings to (coworkers / clients / customers / potential customers / vendors / subcontractors).
3. Many of my business contacts live in (the US / Canada / the UK / India / China / Germany).

Comprehension Check Answers
1. Ken is thanking Nat for being an amazing business partner.
2. He is looking forward to continuing to work with Nat.

Vocabulary Answers
1. c, 2. d, 3. a, 4. b, 5. f, 6. e

Vocab Test Answers
1. Best wishes, 2. amazing, 3. business partner, 4. warmest greetings, 5. continue to, 6. holiday season

Grammar Points Answers
1. a) Christmas season b) the coming year c) the winter holidays
2. a) client b) manager c) accountant

Editing Sentences Answer
① say → send

Real Writing Sample Answer
Scenario 1
Subject: Best wishes!

Dear Dean,

We wanted to send you our warmest greetings and best wishes for the holiday season. It's been an amazing year. You've been a wonderful client. We look forward to working with you for many more years.

Regards,

Barry

Homework Sample Answer
Subject: Happy holidays!

Hi Gloria,

Happy holidays! We wanted to send you our warmest greetings and best wishes. It's been a wonderful year. You've been a fabulous colleague. We look forward to seeing you at the Christmas party. Let's all get into the holiday spirit!

Regards,

Janice

Writing Tip

Respecting Cultural Differences
문화 차이 존중하기

We often work with people from different cultures. Even if we can communicate well in English, miscommunications and misunderstandings can still occur. This is due to cultural differences.
우리는 자주 다른 문화에서 온 사람들과 함께 일하게 된다. 영어로 의사소통이 잘 될 수 있다 하더라도 의사소통에서 오류와 오해가 여전히 생길 수 있다. 이는 문화 차이 때문이다.

① Don't make assumptions. 지레 추측하지 않는다.

Realize that people from different cultures have different values and belief systems. For example, you might not want to say "Merry Christmas!" to people who do not celebrate Christmas for religious reasons. "Happy holidays" may be a more appropriate choice, and wishing them a "Good winter break" is the safest if you are unsure.

다른 문화에서 온 사람들은 다른 가치와 신념 체계를 가지고 있음을 인지한다. 예를 들어, 종교적 이유로 크리스마스를 기념하지 않는 사람들에게 '즐거운 크리스마스 되세요!'라고 하지 않는다. '겨울 연휴 기간 즐겁게 보내세요'가 더 적절한 선택일 수 있고, 확실하지 않을 때는 '좋은 겨울 휴가 보내세요'라고 하는 게 가장 안전하다.

② Be open-minded. 열린 마음을 가진다.

Let's say you see someone acting differently. It is easy to think they are acting strange. You might think they have some problem. It's important not to comment on behavior that you do not understand. Seek to learn rather than judge.

다르게 행동하는 사람을 봤다고 가정하자. 이때 이 사람이 이상하게 행동한다고 생각하기 쉽다. 문제가 있는 사람으로 간주할 수도 있다. 내가 이해하지 못하는 행동에 대해 지적하지 않는 것이 중요하다. 판단하는 것보다 배워야 한다.

③ Recognize that we're different. 우리는 다 다르다는 것을 인지한다.

Be aware of the differences between cultures. Respect those differences. Your culture is valid. So is everybody else's. Avoid saying or writing anything that might sound like you are putting a culture down.

문화 차이가 존재한다는 것을 인지한다. 이런 차이를 존중한다. 내 문화는 타당하다. 타인의 문화도 타당하다. 그 문화를 깎아내리는 듯한 말이나 글을 피한다.

PAGODA
BUSINESS
BIBLE

Basic

PRESENTATION

1 Starting a Presentation

 Learning Objectives

- Learners can greet the audience.
- Learners can thank the audience for coming.
- Learners can introduce themselves.

 Warm Up

Work with a partner or in a group. Discuss the following questions.
1. When was the last time you gave a presentation?
2. Why do people give presentations at work?
3. What should you do to give a great presentation?

Structure

A presentation consists of an introduction, body, and conclusion. In some cases, there is a separate Q&A section.

프레젠테이션의 구성 요소

인사	▶ Welcome the audience and thank them for coming. 청중을 환영하고 감사의 인사를 전한다.	
	Good evening! Thank you all for being here. 안녕하세요! 이 자리에 참석해 주셔서 감사합니다.	
소개	▶ Introduce yourself. Depending on the situation, you can give some information about your background. 자기소개를 한다. 상황에 따라, 나에 대한 정보를 제공할 수 있다.	
	I'm Debra Conner. I'm a marketing manager at ABC Corp. 저는 Debra Conner입니다. ABC 사의 마케팅 매니저입니다.	
주제, 목적	▶ State the topic and purpose of the presentation. 프레젠테이션의 주제와 목적이 무엇인지 설명한다.	
	Today, I'm excited to tell you about our new marketing campaign in Europe. 오늘은 유럽에서 저희의 새로운 마케팅 캠페인에 대해 말씀드리게 되어 기쁩니다.	
	The purpose of today's presentation is to give you a clear understanding of our marketing campaign. 오늘 프레젠테이션의 목적은 저희 마케팅 캠페인에 대한 명확한 이해를 돕기 위함입니다.	
이익	▶ You can also tell the audience what they can gain from the presentation. 청중이 프레젠테이션을 통해 무엇을 얻을 수 있는지 설명할 수 있다.	
	You'll have a clear understanding of our marketing campaign. 저희 마케팅 캠페인에 대해 명확하게 이해하시게 될 것입니다.	
개요	▶ Outline the main points of the presentation. 프레젠테이션의 요점을 요약한다.	
	First, I'll talk about the European market. 먼저, 유럽 시장에 대해 말씀드리겠습니다.	
	Second, I'll show you the overall concept of our marketing campaign. And third, … 둘째, 저희 마케팅 캠페인의 전반적인 콘셉트를 보여드리겠습니다. 그리고 셋째, …	
본론	▶ Explore the main points outlined earlier in depth. 앞에서 소개한 요점을 자세히 살펴본다.	
	Let's begin with the European market. It's a great place to introduce our products. 유럽 시장부터 보겠습니다. 저희 제품을 소개하기에 아주 좋은 곳입니다.	
마무리	▶ You can either recap the main points of your presentation or include a call to action for the audience. 프레젠테이션의 요점을 요약하거나 다음으로 해야 할 일을 알려줄 수 있다.	
	Let's recap the key points we've discussed today. 오늘 논의한 주요 내용을 요약해 보겠습니다.	
	I encourage you all to join us by signing up today. 오늘 가입하셔서 저희와 함께하시길 권합니다.	
Q&A	▶ As an option, open up a Q&A session for the audience to ask questions. 청중이 질문할 수 있도록 Q&A 세션을 진행해 볼 수 있다.	
	If you have any questions, feel free to share them now. 질문이 있으시면 바로 말씀해 주세요.	

Sample Presentation Script

Read the presentation aloud.

Good morning, everyone!

Thank you all for coming. I'm really excited to be here this morning.

Before we begin, **I'd like to take some time to introduce myself.** My name is Greg Nelson. I am the Director of Sales at PlayToys, Inc. I have been with the company for more than eight years.

This morning, I'm here to share some exciting news.

좋은 아침입니다, 여러분!

여기 와 주신 모든 분께 감사드립니다. 오전부터 이 자리에 서 있으니 정말 기쁩니다.

시작하기 전에, **잠시 제 소개할 시간을 갖도록 하겠습니다.** 제 이름은 Greg Nelson입니다. 저는 PlayToys 사의 영업 이사입니다. 저는 이 회사에서 8년 넘게 일해왔습니다.

신나는 소식을 전해드리기 위해 오늘 아침 이 자리에 섰습니다.

✓ Comprehension Check

Answer the questions.

1. Who is Greg Nelson?
2. How long has he been with the company?

Vocabulary

Match the words or expressions with the correct definitions.

1. really excited _____
2. this morning _____
3. take some time _____
4. more than _____
5. share _____
6. exciting news _____

a. 전하다, 공유하다
b. 시간을 내다, 시간을 들이다
c. ~넘게, ~보다 많이
d. 신나는 소식
e. 정말 기쁜
f. 오늘 아침

✓ Vocab Test

Fill in the blanks with the correct words or expressions.

> really excited / this morning / take some time / more than / share / exciting news

1. I want to _____ some good news.
2. I'm _____ to see you all.
3. _____ to think about this.
4. That is _____.
5. The e-mail came in _____.
6. There are _____ two people here.

⊕ Bonus Resources

(an) air of excitement 들뜬 분위기

A: Wow, I sense **an air of excitement** here. 와, 여기 들뜬 분위기가 느껴집니다.
B: Sure. The new CEO will be speaking soon. 맞아요. 신임 CEO께서 곧 연설하실 겁니다.

air는 원래 '공기', '대기' 등을 뜻하지만, 여기서는 '분위기'를 말한다. '흥분'을 일컫는 excitement가 담긴 분위기라는 의미로 쓰이는 긍정적인 표현이다.

Grammar Points

Read the following and practice making sentences.

1. Thank you all for ~

> Thank you all for ~는 '~에 여러분 모두에게 감사드립니다'라는 뜻으로, 행사에 참여한 모든 이에게 특정 행동에 대한 감사를 전할 때 쓸 수 있는 아주 유용한 표현이다.
>
> ✉ *Thank you all for* your outstanding work. 훌륭한 업무 처리에 여러분 모두에게 감사드립니다.

a) Thank you all for _____. 이것을 해 주셔서 여러분 모두에게 감사드립니다.
b) Thank you all for _____ the meeting. 회의에 참석해 주신 여러분 모두에게 감사드립니다.
c) Thank you all for _____. 함께 일해주신 여러분 모두에게 감사드립니다.

2. I'd like to take some time to ~

> I'd like to ~는 I would like to의 줄임말로 '~하고 싶다'라는 말의 격식 표현이다. 친한 친구와 말할 때는 I want to라고 하는 것이 더 자연스럽다. 또한, take some time은 '시간을 들이다'라는 의미로, to 뒤에 동사가 오면 '시간을 내어 ~하고 싶다'라는 뜻이다.
>
> ✉ *I'd like to take some time to* think about your offer. 시간을 내어 당신의 제안에 대해 생각해 보고 싶습니다.

a) I'd like to take some time to _____ this e-mail. 시간을 내어 이 이메일을 읽어보고 싶습니다.
b) I'd like to take some time to _____ it with my boss.
   시간을 내어 저의 상사와 논의해 보고 싶습니다.
c) I'd like to take some time to _____ your proposal.
   시간을 내어 당신의 제안서를 검토해 보고 싶습니다.

Practice

Practice writing sentences. Use the given words or use your own. Then, read your sentences to your partner or group.

1. I'm excited to ~

   (present my work / give my presentation / talk about our new service)

   - _____
   - _____
   - _____

2. I have been ~

   (working here for three years / waiting for 30 minutes / leading this project)

   - _____
   - _____
   - _____

Write

Write a short presentation script that introduces you or someone else.

_____

_____

_____

 Real Presentation

Read the scenario and the four key items on the flashcard. Then, do a short beginning of a presentation welcoming the audience and introducing yourself. When another member of your group presents, use the checklist below.

Scenario

> You are the CEO of an American supermarket chain called Winsome Foods. You are giving a presentation to investors about your company and the new stores that are opening soon. Winsome Foods was founded 20 years ago. You have some great news to share.

Flashcard

1. Jennifer Koh - CEO of Winsome Foods	**2.** national supermarket chain in the U.S.
3. with the company for 20 years	**4.** some great news

✓ Presentation Checklist	Y	N
The presenter made eye contact with the audience.		
The presenter used gestures and body language.		
The presenter spoke clearly and confidently.		
The presenter correctly used words/expressions from the lesson.		

185

Homework

You are speaking to some potential clients. Write a short beginning of a presentation welcoming the audience and introducing yourself. Then, record yourself giving the presentation. Listen to your recording and think about how you can improve your presentation.

___

Warm Up Sample Answers
1. The last time I gave a presentation was (when I was in college / last year / two months ago).
2. People give presentations at work to (share results / sell products).
3. You should (have a good main point / speak loudly).

Comprehension Check Answers
1. Greg Nelson is the Director of Sales at PlayToys, Inc.
2. He has been with the company for more than eight years.

Vocabulary Answers
1. e, 2. f, 3. b, 4. c, 5. a, 6. d

Vocab Test Answers
1. share, 2. really excited, 3. Take some time, 4. exciting news, 5. this morning, 6. more than

Grammar Points Answers
1. a) doing this b) attending / coming to c) working together
2. a) read b) discuss c) review

Write Sample Answer
Good morning, everyone!
I'd like to take some time to introduce my boss, Michael Foster. Michael is our Director of Customer Service. He's been with the company for five years, and he is a fantastic leader.

Real Presentation Sample Answer
Good evening, everyone.
Thank you all for coming. I'm really glad to see everyone.
Before we get started, I'd like to take some time to introduce myself. My name is Jennifer Koh. I'm the CEO of Winsome Foods, a national supermarket chain in the U.S. I've been with the company for 20 years.
Today, I'm here to give you some great news.

Homework Sample Answer
Good afternoon, everyone!
Thank you all for coming. I'm thrilled to be here. I can sense an air of excitement.
Before we begin, I'd like to take some time to tell you about myself. My name is Patrick Horace. I'm a sales manager at Wonderful Gadgets. I've been with the company for more than five years.
Today, I'm here to talk about some great products.

> **Presentation Tip**

How to Lighten the Mood at the Beginning of Your Presentation
프레젠테이션 시작할 때 분위기를 띄우는 방법

You are ready to start your presentation. You might want to lighten the mood with your audience. To do that, you can talk about the following topics.
프레젠테이션을 시작할 준비가 되었다. 청중과 함께 분위기를 밝게 하고 싶을 수 있다. 이를 위해 다음과 같은 주제에 대해 이야기해 볼 수 있다.

① The weather 날씨

You can easily break the ice by bringing up a lighthearted topic. For example, you can talk about the weather before talking about a serious topic.
가벼운 주제를 꺼내면 분위기를 쉽게 띄울 수 있다. 예를 들어, 진지한 주제에 대해 이야기하기 전에 날씨를 언급할 수 있다.

- *It's hot outside, isn't it? I was outside for just five minutes, and I was already sweating.*
  오늘 날씨가 덥네요, 그렇죠? 밖에 5분 나갔다 왔는데도 이미 땀을 흘리고 있었어요.

② An audience member 참석자

Sometimes you see an important or a well-known person in the audience. Go ahead and mention them to the audience. This way, you can draw attention to what you're saying. It's also a simple, easy way of getting people to focus on you.
때로는 청중 중에 중요하거나 잘 알려진 사람이 있을 수 있다. 그럴 때는 청중에게 그 사람을 언급해 본다. 그러면 발표에 주의를 끌 수 있다. 이는 사람들이 나에게 집중하게 할 수 있는 간단하고 쉬운 방법이기도 하다.

- *I see Dr. Brown is here today. As you all know, he's an expert in our field. Let's hope he doesn't find my presentation too boring.*
  오늘 Brown 박사님이 오셨군요. 여러분도 아시다시피 그분이 저희 분야의 전문가이죠. 그분이 제 프레젠테이션을 너무 지루해하시지 않기를 바라겠습니다.

③ A funny story or joke 재미있는 이야기 또는 농담

You can make a joke. It's a good way to make the audience laugh and help them relax.
농담을 던져볼 수 있다. 청중을 웃게 하고 긴장을 풀어줄 수 있는 좋은 방법이다.

- *You know, everyone is on a diet these days. Vegetarian, Keto – so many different diets. So I decided to try one. It's called the "FCB" diet. It's short for the "Fried Chicken and Beer" diet.*
  요즘은 모두가 다이어트를 하고 있습니다. 채식주의자, 케토 등 정말 다양한 다이어트가 있죠. 그래서 저는 하나를 시도하기로 했습니다. 일명 'FCB' 다이어트입니다. '프라이드치킨과 맥주' 다이어트의 줄임말이죠.

2 Stating the Topic and Main Points

 Learning Objectives

- Learners can state the topic of their presentation.
- Learners can state the purpose of their presentation as needed.
- Learners can outline the main points of their presentation.

 Warm Up

Work with a partner or in a group. Discuss the following questions.

1. What are most of your presentations about?
2. In general, how many main points should a presentation have?
3. What type of presentation may not need an outline of main points?

Sample Presentation Script

Read the presentation aloud.

Today, I'll be talking about BeeOn, our new AI drone for kids.

First, I'll tell you about BeeOn's distinct features. Next, I'll go over BeeOn's user-friendly mobile app. Finally, we will look at the various accessories for BeeOn.

By the end of the talk, you'll see all the reasons why I'm so excited about BeeOn.

All right, then. Let's get started.

오늘은 아이들을 위한 최신 제품인 AI 드론인 BeeOn에 대해 말씀드리겠습니다.

먼저, BeeOn의 뚜렷한 특징에 대해 알려드리겠습니다. 그다음에는 사용하기 편한 BeeOn의 모바일 앱에 대해 설명하겠습니다. 마지막으로 BeeOn의 다양한 액세서리를 함께 보겠습니다.

프레젠테이션이 끝날 때쯤이면 제가 BeeOn에 대해 열광하는 이유를 아시게 될 겁니다.

자, 그럼 시작해 보겠습니다.

✓ Comprehension Check

Answer the questions.

1. What is BeeOn?
2. How many main points are there?

Vocabulary

Match the words or expressions with the correct definitions.

1. distinct _____
2. feature _____
3. go over _____
4. user-friendly _____
5. look at _____
6. various _____

a. ~을 설명하다, ~을 다루다
b. ~을 보다, ~을 살펴보다
c. 뚜렷한
d. 다양한, 여러 가지의
e. 사용하기 편한, 사용자 친화적
f. 특징

✓ Vocab Test

Fill in the blanks with the correct words or expressions.

distinct / feature / go over / user-friendly / look at / various

1. The software is not complicated at all. It is very _____.
2. There is a _____ resemblance between the two products.
3. Wow, _____ that nice building.
4. Josie has held _____ positions at this company.
5. Is this a new _____ ?
6. Let's _____ the report.

⊕ Bonus Resources

give a rundown 상황에 대해 간략하게 요약하다

A: What are you going to talk about in your presentation?
프레젠테이션에서 무슨 말씀하실 건가요?
B: I'm going to **give a rundown** of our company's history.
회사의 역사에 대해 요약할 겁니다.

rundown은 20세기 초반에 '경마 출전마 목록 및 배당률 정보'라는 의미로 쓰였다. 현재는 속어로 '요약'이라는 뜻이다. 구어체 표현으로, 일상 회화에서 자주 사용한다.

 **Grammar Points**

Read the following and practice making sentences.

1. I'll be talking about ~

> I'll은 I will의 줄임말로 '~하겠다'는 뜻으로 I'll be talking about ~은 말 그대로 '~에 대해 말하겠다'를 의미한다. 어떤 주제든지 이 패턴을 써서 프레젠테이션 뒷부분에서 다루고자 하는 것을 언급하면 된다.
>
> *I'll be talking about the new company policy.* 새로운 회사 방침에 대해 말씀드리겠습니다.

a) I'll be talking about _____. 저희의 새로운 서비스에 대해 말씀드리겠습니다.

b) I'll be talking about _____. 프로젝트에 대해 말씀드리겠습니다.

c) I'll be talking about _____ of our company. 당사의 역사에 대해 말씀드리겠습니다.

2. By the end of the talk, you'll ~

> By the end of the talk, you'll ~은 '프레젠테이션이 끝나면, ~하실 겁니다'를 뜻하며, 뒤에는 동사 원형이 붙는다. 참고로 presentation 대신 talk라는 단어도 자주 쓴다.
>
> *By the end of the presentation, you'll know how to build one.*
> 프레젠테이션이 끝나면, 어떻게 하나로 만드는지 아시게 될 겁니다.

a) By the end of the talk, you'll _____ our position.
   프레젠테이션이 끝나면, 저희 입장을 이해하시게 될 겁니다.

b) By the end of the presentation, you'll _____ next.
   프레젠테이션이 끝나면, 다음에 무엇을 해야 할지 아시게 될 겁니다.

c) By the end of the talk, you'll _____ a better understanding of the policy.
   프레젠테이션이 끝나면, 방침에 대해 더 잘 이해하시게 될 겁니다.

 **Practice**

Making Sentences

Practice writing sentences. Use the given words or use your own. Then, read your sentences to your partner or group.

1. I'll go over ~

    (the new data / the report / the benefits)

    - _____
    - _____
    - _____

2. All right, then. Let's ~

    (go to lunch / start the meeting / wrap it up)

    - _____
    - _____
    - _____

Write

Write a short presentation script that states the topic and outlines main points.

_____
_____
_____

Real Presentation

Read the scenario and the four key items on the flashcard. Then, do a short beginning of a presentation stating the topic and outlining the main points. When another member of your group presents, use the checklist below.

Scenario

> You are a manager at your company's HR division. You are giving a presentation to the other department managers about your company's new vacation policy. Your main points are the differences between the old and the new one, the main reason for the change, and the implementation date. By the end of the presentation, the audience will get a general overview of the new policy.

Flashcard

1. new vacation policy	**2.** differences between the old and new policy
3. the main reason for the change	**4.** the implementation date

✓ Presentation Checklist	Y	N
The presenter made eye contact with the audience.		
The presenter used gestures and body language.		
The presenter spoke clearly and confidently.		
The presenter correctly used words/expressions from the lesson.		

Homework

You are speaking to your project team. Write a short beginning of a presentation stating the topic and outlining the main points. Then, record yourself giving the presentation. Listen to your recording and think about how you can improve your presentation.

___
___
___

Warm Up Sample Answers
1. Most of my presentations are about (projects / products / our services).
2. A presentation should have (about three / only two / less than three) points.
3. A presentation (that is very short / about a single topic) may not need an outline of main points.

Comprehension Check Answers
1. BeeOn is a new AI drone for kids.
2. There are three main points.

Vocabulary Answers
1. c, 2. f, 3. a, 4. e, 5. b, 6. d

Vocab Test Answers
1. user-friendly, 2. distinct, 3. look at, 4. various, 5. feature, 6. go over

Grammar Points Answers
1. a) our new service b) the project c) the history
2. a) understand b) know what to do c) have

Write Sample Answer
I'll be talking about the new messenger app.
First, I'll go over the reasons for implementing the app. Next, we'll look at some of its features.
By the end of the talk, you'll have a general understanding of the app.

Real Presentation Sample Answer
Today, I'll be talking about the new vacation policy.
First, I'll discuss the differences between the old and the new one. Next, I'll go over the main reason for the change. Finally, we'll look at the implementation date.
By the end of the talk, you'll get a general overview of the policy.
All right, then. Let's start.

Homework Sample Answer
I'll be talking about the new project in Singapore.
First, I'll give a rundown of the scope and budget. Next, I'll go over the staffing. Finally, we'll look at the schedule.
By the end of the talk, you'll have a good grasp of the Singapore project.
All right, then. Let's get started, shall we?

Presentation Tip

Important Things to Consider about Your Audience
청중에 대해 고려해야 할 중요한 사항

Each presentation should cater to a specific audience. To do so, consider the following:
프레젠테이션마다 특정한 청중에 맞추어야 한다. 이를 위해 다음을 고려해 보자:

① Size and background 규모와 배경

Think about the size and the background of the audience. How many people are expected to attend? How are they related to one another? For example, are they all from the same company? What are their positions? Do they all speak English fluently? You will need to customize your presentation to the specific audience.

청중의 규모와 배경을 생각해 본다. 몇 명이 참석할 것으로 예상하는가? 서로 어떤 관계인가? 예를 들어, 모두 같은 회사 사람들인가? 직책이 무엇인가? 모두 영어가 유창한가? 프레젠테이션을 특정 청중에게 맞추어야 한다.

② Attitude 태도

Consider the audience's attitude toward the topic. Will they be interested, or will they be apathetic? They may even be hostile. Decide what type of supporting material you will need. You might need to prepare extra data, samples, or photos.

주제에 대한 청중의 태도를 고려한다. 관심을 가질 것인가, 아니면 무관심할 것인가? 적대적일 수도 있다. 뒷받침할 필요한 자료가 무엇인지 정한다. 추가 데이터나 샘플, 또는 사진을 준비해 볼 수 있다.

③ Existing knowledge 기존 지식

The audience's prior knowledge is also important. Are they already somewhat knowledgeable? If so, you can skip certain elements of the topic. You can also use the words and expressions they will know. If they are not knowledgeable, you will need to use simpler language. You should also give more details.

청중의 사전 지식도 중요하다. 이미 어느 정도의 지식이 있는가? 그렇다면 일부 부분을 생략할 수 있다. 그들이 아는 단어와 표현을 쓸 수도 있다. 만약 그들이 아는 것이 많지 않다면, 더 쉬운 언어를 사용해야 한다. 자세하게 설명해 줘야 한다.

3 Entertaining the Audience

 Learning Objectives

- Learners can pique the audience's attention with stories.
- Learners can tell stories that are relevant to the topic.
- Learners can use appropriate language for entertaining the audience.

 Warm Up

Work with a partner or in a group. Discuss the following questions.

1. Do you normally try to entertain the audience during a presentation?
2. What are some ways to entertain the audience?
3. Should you always try to entertain the audience? Why or why not?

Sample Presentation Script

Read the presentation aloud.

My name is Yoojin. I used to think it was a very feminine name.

Then something happened that made me realize that was only in Korea.

One day, I went to the office of a potential client. I had made the appointment with his secretary. When he saw me, suddenly there was an awkward silence. He looked really surprised. You see, he was expecting somebody with a name that sounded like mine, just not a woman named Yoojin. He was expecting a man named Eugene.

저의 이름은 Yoojin입니다. 아주 여성스러운 이름으로 생각하곤 했습니다.

그런데 그런 생각이 한국에서만 그렇다는 걸 깨닫게 한 일이 벌어졌습니다.

한번은 어떤 잠재적 고객의 사무실로 갔습니다. 그의 비서와 약속을 잡았었죠. 그가 저를 봤을 때 갑자기 어색한 침묵이 흘렀습니다. 그는 무척 놀란 듯 보였습니다. 그러니까, Yoojin이라는 여자를 기다렸던 것이 아니라 저와 비슷한 이름을 가진 사람을 기다렸던 거죠. 그는 남자 Eugene을 기다리고 있었습니다.

✓ Comprehension Check

Answer the questions.

1. What did the speaker use to think about her name?
2. Whose office did the speaker go to?

Vocabulary

Match the words or expressions with the correct definitions.

1. used to _____	a. 여성스러운
2. feminine _____	b. ~하곤 했다
3. potential _____	c. 어색한
4. awkward _____	d. 단지 ~아닌
5. you see _____	e. 그러니까, 있잖아요
6. just not _____	f. 잠재적

✓ Vocab Test

Fill in the blanks with the correct words or expressions.

used to / feminine / potential / awkward / you see / just not

1. She is a _____ customer.
2. This is an _____ situation.
3. I _____ like coffee but not anymore.
4. _____, I have to leave now.
5. I like pizza, _____ pepperoni pizza.
6. The book cover had a _____ look.

⊕ Bonus Resources

sweat bullets 몹시 불안하거나 걱정을 하다

A: How was your presentation? 당신의 프레젠테이션은 어땠어요?
B: I was **sweating bullets**, but I think I did okay.
   굉장히 걱정했는데, 괜찮게 한 것 같아요.

크게 염려하거나 아주 불안한 상태일 때 땀이 많이 나기 마련이다. 이 표현은 땀방울이 하도 커서 bullet, 즉 '총알' 크기라는 우스꽝스러운 표현에서 나왔다는 설이 있다.

 **Grammar Points**

Read the following and practice making sentences.

1. Something happened that ~

> Something happened that ~은 '~하게 한 일이 생겼다'를 뜻한다. 이미 생긴 일인 만큼, 뒤에는 과거형 동사가 붙는다는 것을 기억하자.
>
> 📖 *Something happened that changed my opinion about work.*
>   일에 대한 제 생각이 바뀌게 한 일이 벌어졌습니다.

a) Something happened that _____ strange. 이상하게 보이는 일이 벌어졌습니다.

b) Something happened that _____ the CEO. CEO를 화나게 한 일이 벌어졌습니다.

c) Something happened that _____ my perspective.
   저의 관점을 완전히 바꾸게 한 일이 벌어졌습니다.

2. One day, I ~

> 직역하면 '하루는 제가 ~'를 말하지만, '한번은 제가 ~'의 의미가 더 가깝다. 과거 한 시점에서 내가 경험했던 특정한 상황 전개하고자 할 때 유용한 표현이다.
>
> 📖 *One day, I attended an important project meeting.* 한번은 중요한 프로젝트 회의에 참여했습니다.

a) One day, I _____ lunch with my boss. 한번은 저의 상사와 점심 먹으러 나갔습니다.

b) One day, I _____ an e-mail from John. 한번은 John에게서 이메일을 받았습니다.

c) One day, I _____ a day off from work. 한번은 일일 휴가를 냈습니다.

 **Practice**

Making Sentences

Practice writing sentences. Use the given words or use your own. Then, read your sentences to your partner or group.

1. I used to ~

    (live in Daejeon / drive to work / have a PC)

    - _____
    - _____
    - _____

2. He looked really ~

    (unhappy / pleased / worried)

    - _____
    - _____
    - _____

Write

Write a short presentation script that tells an entertaining story about a time you were embarrassed about something.

_____
_____
_____

Real Presentation

Read the scenario and the four key items on the flashcard. Then, tell the audience about a time you made a mistake. When another member of your group presents, use the checklist below.

Scenario

> You are a manager. You are giving a light presentation to your staff to tell them it's okay to make mistakes. You are now telling them about a time you went to an auto show with a friend. You used to think you knew a lot about cars. While looking at a car, you asked a rep where the gas tank was. It turned out the car was electric, not gasoline-powered.

Flashcard

1. used to think I knew about cars	2. an auto show with a friend
3. ask: where is the gas tank?	4. it was an electric car

✓ Presentation Checklist	Y	N
The presenter made eye contact with the audience.		
The presenter used gestures and body language.		
The presenter spoke clearly and confidently.		
The presenter correctly used words/expressions from the lesson.		

Homework

You are speaking to coworkers at a company retreat. Write a short part of a presentation telling the audience about changing a routine. Then, record yourself giving the presentation. Listen to your recording and think about how you can improve your presentation.

Warm Up Sample Answers
1. (Yes, I / No, I don't) normally try to entertain the audience.
2. I can (tell a joke / tell a funny story / show an interesting slide).
3. Yes, because it makes presentations more effective. / No, because some presentations are about very serious topics.

Comprehension Check Answers
1. She used to think her name was a very feminine name.
2. The speaker went to a potential client's office.

Vocabulary Answers
1. b, 2. a, 3. f, 4. c, 5. e, 6. d

Vocab Test Answers
1. potential, 2. awkward, 3. used to, 4. You see, 5. just not, 6. feminine

Grammar Points Answers
1. a) seemed/looked b) upset/angered c) completely/totally changed
2. a) went to b) received/got c) took

Write Sample Answer
Something happened that really embarrassed me.
One day, I called a colleague on the phone. His name is Jose. I greeted him but pronounced his name wrong. I said, "Hello, Joss." I should have used the Spanish pronunciation.

Real Presentation Sample Answer
I used to think that I knew a lot about cars.
Then something happened that changed my mind.
One day, I went to an auto show with a friend. We saw a fantastic sports car. I asked the rep where the gas tank was. He looked surprised. You see, it was an electric car!

Homework Sample Answer
I used to drive to work.
Then something happened that changed this routine.
One day, I drove to work as usual. Suddenly, it began to snow! I was sweating bullets. You see, I don't like driving in the snow. It snowed a lot. I arrived two hours late. My boss looked really upset.
Now I take the bus and subway to work.

Presentation Tip

Ways to Hook Your Audience
청중의 관심을 끄는 방법

①
A story 이야기

People love stories. A story gets the audience interested. You become relatable. If possible, tell a story about yourself.
사람들은 이야기를 좋아한다. 이야기는 청중의 관심을 끈다. 나와 공감대를 형성하게 해준다. 가능하다면, 나에 대한 이야기도 들려주자.

 Let me start with a story about a manager. That manager is me. Something happened two weeks ago that changed how I work.
어느 매니저에 대한 이야기로 시작하겠습니다. 그 매니저는 접니다. 2주 전에 제가 일하는 방식을 바꿔 놓은 일이 있었습니다.

②
A video 동영상

A video can act as an ice breaker. You might start your presentation with a video. Make sure that it is related to your topic. Also, keep the running time short.
비디오는 아이스브레이킹 역할을 할 수 있다. 비디오로 프레젠테이션을 시작할 수 있다. 반드시 나의 주제와 관련되어야 한다. 재생 시간을 짧게 하자.

 Okay, that was a video we shot last month. The factory you saw is our own factory in Ulsan.
네, 저희가 지난달에 찍은 영상이었습니다. 보신 공장은 울산에 있는 저희 공장입니다.

③
A rhetorical question 수사 의문문

A rhetorical question is not meant to be answered. It is almost like a statement. It is meant to get your audience thinking.
수사 의문문은 답변을 요구하지 않는다. 거의 진술이나 마찬가지다. 청중이 생각하도록 유도하기 위함이다.

 Are freight costs too high? Many of our clients say so. You might be paying too much right now, in fact.
수송비가 너무 많이 드나요? 많은 고객이 그렇다고 합니다. 사실 여러분은 지금 아주 많은 돈을 내고 있을 수 있습니다.

④
A quote 명언

Find an interesting quote by a famous person. It should be related to your topic. Put the quote and a photo on a slide.
유명한 사람의 명언을 찾아본다. 나의 주제와 관련이 있어야 한다. 슬라이드에 명언과 사진을 함께 올린다.

 This is Steve Jobs. He said: "Great things in business are never done by one person. They're done by a team of people."
이분은 Steve Jobs입니다. 이런 말을 했죠. '비즈니스에서 위대한 일은 결코 한 사람이 이룰 수 없습니다. 한 팀의 사람들에 의해 이루어지는 것이죠.'

4 Using Transitions

 Learning Objectives

- Learners can use transitions to conclude a section.
- Learners can use transitions to start a new section.
- Learners can use transitions to list separate ideas.

 Warm Up

Work with a partner or in a group. Discuss the following questions.

1. Is using transitions important when making presentations?
2. Do you find it difficult using proper transitions when making presentations?
3. What are some examples of transitions?

Sample Presentation Script

Read the presentation aloud.

> **That's all on the background.**
>
> **Now, let's move on to the training program.**
>
> There are three aspects to the program. The first one is the diverse curriculum. The second one is the instructors for each of the courses. And the third one is the employees who are eligible for those courses.
>
> So, let's look at the first aspect: the curriculum.

그것으로 배경을 다 다루었습니다.

이제, 훈련 프로그램으로 넘어가겠습니다.

해당 프로그램에는 세 가지 측면이 있습니다. 첫 번째는 커리큘럼의 다양성입니다. 두 번째는 각 과정의 강사입니다. 그리고 세 번째는 그 과정을 이수할 자격이 있는 직원입니다.

자, 첫 번째 측면인 커리큘럼을 보겠습니다.

✓ Comprehension Check

Answer the questions.

1. What topic is the speaker moving on to?
2. How many aspects are there?

 **Vocabulary**

Match the words or expressions with the correct definitions.

1. background _____
2. move on to _____
3. aspect _____
4. diverse _____
5. curriculum _____
6. eligible _____

a. 배경
b. 측면
c. 다양한, 다양성 있는
d. 교육과정
e. ~으로 넘어가다
f. ~할 자격이 있는

Vocab Test

Fill in the blanks with the correct words or expressions.

background / move on to / aspects / diverse / curriculum / eligible

1. There are four _____ to the policy.
2. All employees are _____.
3. John has an engineering _____.
4. Cindy has a _____ range of skills.
5. Let me _____ a different topic.
6. The workshop has a great _____.

⊕ Bonus Resources

jump right in 바로 시작하다

A: We need to discuss the project in Osan.
오산에 있는 프로젝트에 대해 논의해야 합니다.

B: I agree. Let's **jump right in** and talk about it.
동의합니다. 바로 시작해서 얘기해 보죠.

jump in이라고 하면 '뛰어들어'로 직역되는데, right를 jump in 사이에 넣으면 '바로 뛰어들어'가 된다. 무언가를 지체하지 말고 행동으로 옮기자는 뜻이다.

Grammar Points

Read the following and practice making sentences.

1. That's all on ~

> That's all on ~은 That is all on의 줄임말로, '~에 대해 그것이 다입니다'로 직역되며, '그것으로 ~을 다 다루었다'라는 뜻이다. 한 소주제를 마칠 때 보내는 신호로, 프레젠테이션에서 매우 유용한 표현이다.
>
> *That's all on last year's sales figures.* 그것으로 작년 매출액을 다 다루었습니다.

a) That's all on _____. 그것으로 일본 시장을 다 다루었습니다.

b) That's all on _____. 그것으로 새로운 색상을 다 다루었습니다.

c) That's all on _____. 그것으로 혜택을 다 다루었습니다.

2. Let's move on to ~

> Let's move on to ~는 Let us move on to의 줄임말로, '~로 넘어갑시다'를 의미한다. move on이라는 말에서 볼 수 있듯, 한 소주제를 마친 다음에 다른 소주제로 넘어갈 때 자주 사용하는 표현이다.
>
> *Let's move on to this year's sales figures.* 올해 매출액으로 넘어가겠습니다.

a) Let's move on to _____. 마지막 항목으로 넘어가겠습니다.

b) Let's move on to _____. 두 가지 디자인으로 넘어가겠습니다.

c) Let's move on to _____. 다음 질문으로 넘어가겠습니다.

Practice

Making Sentences

Practice writing sentences. Use the given words or use your own. Then, read your sentences to your partner or group.

1. The first one is ~

   (the location / the pros and cons / the staffing)

   - _____
   - _____
   - _____

2. Let's look at ~

   (something else / the next slide / the graph)

   - _____
   - _____
   - _____

Write

Write a short presentation script that concludes one item and then moves on to another item.

_____
_____
_____

Real Presentation

Read the scenario and the four key items on the flashcard. Then, do a portion of a presentation where you tell the audience about your company's products. When another member of your group presents, use the checklist below.

Scenario

> You are a sales manager for a book publisher. You are giving a presentation to a small audience at a book fair. You have just talked about science books, and now you are moving on to language learning books. List the three major categories: English, Chinese, and all other languages, including Japanese and Spanish.

Flashcard

1. science books	**2.** moving on to language books
3. three categories: English, Chinese, other languages	**4.** first category: English books

✓ Presentation Checklist	Y	N
The presenter made eye contact with the audience.		
The presenter used gestures and body language.		
The presenter spoke clearly and confidently.		
The presenter correctly used words/expressions from the lesson.		

Homework

You are speaking to some potential clients. Write a short part of a presentation where you tell the audience about your team's main projects. Then, record yourself giving the presentation. Listen to your recording and think about how you can improve your presentation.

_____
_____
_____

Warm Up Sample Answers
1. Yes, using transitions is important. / No, using transitions is not important.
2. (Yes, I / No, I don't) find it difficult.
3. Some examples are (next / now, let's go to / for example).

Comprehension Check Answers
1. The speaker is moving on to the training program.
2. There are three aspects.

Vocabulary Answers
1. a, 2. e, 3. b, 4. c, 5. d, 6. f

Vocab Test Answers
1. aspects, 2. eligible, 3. background, 4. diverse, 5. move on to, 6. curriculum

Grammar Points Answers
1. a) the Japanese market b) the new color c) the benefits
2. a) the last item b) the two designs c) the next question

Write Sample Answer
That's all on the history of our company.
Now, let's move on to our client base.
There are more than fifty major corporate clients currently using our services.

Real Presentation Sample Answer
That's all on the science books.
Let's move on to the language learning books.
There are three major categories. The first one is English learning books. The second one is Chinese learning books. And the third one is all other languages, including Japanese and Spanish.
So, let's look at the first category: English books.

Homework Sample Answer
That's all on the members of the team.
Now, let's move on to some of our projects.
There are three main ones I want to talk about. The first one is the Avery project in Seoul. The second one is the Max Mall project in the Philippines. And the third one is the West Side Complex project in San Diego.
So, let's jump right in and look at the first one: the Avery project.

Presentation Tip

Connecting Your Ideas Effectively Using Transitions
전환을 사용하여 아이디어를 효율적으로 연결하기

It's important to guide your audience from one idea to another. Otherwise, your audience can easily get confused. The best way to avoid that is to use transitions. Of course, you should also use appropriate gestures along with the transitions.

청중을 위해 하나의 주제에서 다른 주제로 연결해 주는 것이 중요하다. 그렇지 않으면 청중은 쉽게 혼란에 빠질 수 있다. 그 문제를 피하는 가장 좋은 방법은 전환을 사용하는 것이다. 물론 전환과 함께 적절한 제스처도 사용하면 좋다.

① Sentences and Paragraphs 문장과 문단

Make smooth transitions between sentences or paragraphs.
문장이나 문단 사이를 부드럽게 잇는다.

 Additional idea 추가 아이디어
Also, In addition, Besides

Opposite idea 반대 아이디어
But, In contrast, However

Result 결과
Therefore, So, That's why

Example 예시
For example, For instance, To give you an example

Emphasis 강조
Especially, In particular, In fact

② Main Sections 주요 부분

You should also link between main sections. When you do, use full sentences.
주요 부분 역시 연결하는 것이 좋다. 그럴 때는 완전한 문장을 사용한다.

That covers Item A. Now, let's move on to Item B. 그걸로 A사항을 다 다뤘습니다. 이제, B사항으로 넘어가죠.
Now that we've looked at Item A, let's go to Item B. A사항을 봤으니, B사항으로 가보겠습니다.

③ Different Items 여러 항목

Use the right transitions when listing multiple items.
다수의 항목을 열거할 때 적절한 전환을 사용한다.

First, Second, Third 첫 번째, 두 번째, 세 번째
First, Next, Then, Finally 먼저, 그다음에, 그런 다음에, 마지막으로
One is..., Another is..., The last one is... 하나는 ~, 또 하나는 ~, 마지막은 ~

5 Giving Supporting Evidence and Examples

 Learning Objectives

- Learners can support the main points of their presentations with supporting evidence.
- Learners can elaborate on the evidence with details.
- Learners can cite specific data or other resources.

 Warm Up

Work with a partner or in a group. Discuss the following questions.
1. What types of evidence can you use when you make a presentation?
2. Do you find yourself needing to present evidence frequently during presentations?
3. What are some good ways to present your evidence?

Sample Presentation Script

Read the presentation aloud.

Our clients love our services.
This is supported by our survey from last year. Over 100 clients participated. An outside consultant was hired to oversee the entire process.

The survey shows that 90% of our clients were satisfied with their experience.

We also asked another question. Would they recommend our services to others? A whopping 95% said yes!

고객들은 저희 서비스에 만족하고 있습니다.
작년에 저희가 진행한 설문조사가 이를 뒷받침합니다. 100명이 넘는 고객들이 참여했습니다. 전체적인 진행을 감독하도록 외부 컨설턴트를 고용했었습니다.

설문조사는 90%가 서비스 경험에 만족하고 있음을 보여주고 있습니다.

고객들에게 또 하나의 질문도 했습니다. 다른 사람들에게 당사 서비스를 추천할 것인가? 무려 95%가 그렇다고 했습니다!

✓ Comprehension Check

Answer the questions.

1. How many clients participated in the survey?
2. What percent of clients were satisfied with their experience?

# Vocabulary

Match the words or expressions with the correct definitions.

1. support _____
2. participate _____
3. outside _____
4. process _____
5. recommend _____
6. whopping _____

a. 참여하다
b. 진행, 과정
c. 뒷받침하다
d. 무려
e. 추천하다
f. 외부

✓ Vocab Test

Fill in the blanks with the correct words or expressions.

supports / participate / outside / process / recommend / whopping

1. Let's hire an _____ engineer.
2. I want to _____ another company.
3. The data _____ their claims.
4. Their CEO received a _____ 200% bonus.
5. Who wants to _____ in the event?
6. The _____ is as important as the goal.

⊕ Bonus Resources

a case in point (상황에) 적절한 사례

A: Is the economy that bad? 경제가 그렇게 안 좋은가요?
B: Yes. **A case in point** is last month's 20% drop in sales.
네, 전월 매출이 20% 하락한 것이 대표적인 예입니다.

a case는 '경우'나 '사례', in point는 '적절한', '해당하는 상황에 맞는'을 뜻한다. 흔히 살짝 격식을 차려 말할 때 쓰이는데, 더 간단하게는 a good example이라고 할 수도 있다.

 **Grammar Points**

Read the following and practice making sentences.

1. **This is supported by ~**

> This is supported by ~는 '~가 이를 뒷받침합니다'를 뜻한다. 여기서 this는 어떤 발언이나 주장을 말하는데, by 뒤에 따르는 명사가 근거나 증거 역할을 한다.
>
> 🔳 *This is supported by a recent article in Night Time.* 〈나이트 타임〉의 최근 기사가 이를 뒷받침합니다.

 a) This is supported by _____ conducted at Harvard.
    하버드대에서 실시한 연구가 이를 뒷받침합니다.

 b) This is supported by _____. 새로운 데이터가 이를 뒷받침합니다.

 c) This is supported by _____. 정부의 연구가 이를 뒷받침합니다.

2. **The survey shows that ~**

> The survey shows that ~은 '설문조사는 ~을 보여줍니다'를 뜻한다. 여기서 '보여주다'를 의미하는 show는 실은 '증명하다'에 더 가깝다.
>
> 🔳 *The survey shows that employees are generally content.*
>   설문조사는 직원들이 대개 만족하고 있음을 보여줍니다.

 a) The survey shows that _____ prefer black.
    설문조사는 응답자 대부분이 검은색을 선호한다는 것을 보여줍니다.

 b) The survey shows that _____ right.
    설문조사는 저희가 맞았다는 것을 보여줍니다.

 c) The survey shows that _____ of managers agree.
    설문조사는 매니저 중 10%만 동의하고 있음을 보여줍니다.

 **Practice**

Making Sentences

Practice writing sentences. Use the given words or use your own. Then, read your sentences to your partner or group.

1. Our clients love ~

    (the new product / the discounts / the ad)

    - _____
    - _____
    - _____

2. Over ~ participated.

    (a hundred people / 20% / thirty employees)

    - _____
    - _____
    - _____

Write

Write a short presentation script that describes what a survey shows in detail.

_____
_____
_____

 **Real Presentation**

Read the scenario and the four key items on the flashcard. Then, do a portion of a presentation where you talk about a recent company survey. When another member of your group presents, use the checklist below.

Scenario

> You are an administrative manager. You are giving a presentation to the executives about a recent employee survey. More than 80% of employees answered the survey. One item is about how the conference rooms are too small. Two-thirds of the respondents want larger conference rooms. The survey also asked how often they have meetings. Sixty-five percent said they have more than two meetings a week.

Flashcard

1. conference rooms are too small	**2.** employee survey with more than 80% of participation
3. 2/3 want larger conference rooms	**4.** 65% have meetings more than twice a week

✓ Presentation Checklist	Y	N
The presenter made eye contact with the audience.		
The presenter used gestures and body language.		
The presenter spoke clearly and confidently.		
The presenter correctly used words/expressions from the lesson.		

 **Homework**

You are speaking to some executives in your company. Write a short part of a presentation where you tell the audience about a recent survey. Then, record yourself giving the presentation. Listen to your recording and think about how you can improve your presentation.

___

___

___

Warm Up Sample Answers
1. I can use (good data / scientific facts / survey results).
2. (Yes, I / No, I don't) find myself needing to do that.
3. Some good ways are to (show a graph / put it on a slide).

Comprehension Check Answers
1. Over 100 clients participated in the survey.
2. Ninety percent of clients were satisfied.

Vocabulary Answers
1. c, 2. a, 3. f, 4. b, 5. e, 6. d

Vocab Test Answers
1. outside, 2. recommend, 3. supports, 4. whopping, 5. participate, 6. process

Grammar Points Answers
1. a) a study b) the new data c) the government's research
2. a) most respondents b) we were c) only 10%

Write Sample Answer
The survey shows that over half of our consumers prefer the new taste. They cited "Sweeter" as the main reason. "More refreshing" was also another reason.

Real Presentation Sample Answer
Our employees think our conference rooms are too small.
This is supported by last month's survey. Over 80% of employees participated.
The survey shows that two-thirds of respondents want larger conference rooms.
We also asked this question: how often do they have meetings? A whopping 65% said more than twice a week.

Homework Sample Answer
Our vendors want better payment terms.
This is supported by a recent survey. Over 20 vendors participated.
The survey shows that more than half of the vendors feel that our payment system is unfair.
A case in point is our net payment term of 60 days.
We asked a specific question. What would be a fair payment term? A whopping 80% said net 30 days.

Presentation Tip

Using Evidence Effectively in Your Presentations
프레젠테이션에서 효율적으로 근거 사용하기

Having good evidence is not enough. You need to use your evidence effectively. Here are some ways to do that.
좋은 근거를 확보한 것만으로는 부족하다. 효율적으로 근거를 사용해야 한다. 그렇게 할 수 있는 방법을 함께 보자.

① Use only two or three pieces of evidence. 근거는 2~3개만 사용한다.

You might have dozens of facts that support your statement or claim. However, giving all that to the audience is overkill. It will only make them tune out. So, select only two or three pieces of evidence that will have the most impact.

나의 의견이나 주장을 뒷받침할 수십 가지의 사실이 있을 수 있다. 하지만 그 모든 것을 청중에게 제공하는 것은 지나치다. 청중이 귀를 기울이지 않게 만들 뿐이다. 그러니 그저 가장 강한 인상을 남길 큰 두세 가지 근거만 선택한다.

② Customize your evidence. 맞춤형 근거를 사용한다.

Choose evidence that matches the scope of your topic. Let's say you're discussing your company's product or services. In this case, testimonials and survey results should be good enough. If you're discussing environmental matters, however, you will need more data.

나의 주제 내용과 맞는 근거를 택한다. 회사의 제품이나 서비스에 대해 언급한다고 치자. 이 경우에는 후기나 설문조사면 충분할 것이다. 하지만 환경 문제에 대한 것이라면 더 많은 데이터가 필요할 것이다.

③ Show the evidence. 근거를 제시한다.

Put the evidence on your presentation slides. People respond well to information that is given visually. Use compelling photos or illustrations. Turn your data into graphs if possible.

프레젠테이션 슬라이드에 근거를 넣자. 사람들은 시각적으로 보여주는 정보에 좋은 반응을 보인다. 흥미진진한 사진이나 삽화를 사용한다. 가능하면 데이터를 도표로 만들자.

④ Check your sources. 출처를 확인한다.

Your information and data must be credible. There's a lot of fake news and inaccurate information online. Also, the data should be recent, not dated.

정보나 데이터는 신뢰가 있어야 한다. 온라인에는 가짜 뉴스와 부정확한 정보가 많다. 더불어 오래되지 않은, 최신의 데이터를 사용하자.

6 Emphasizing Key Points

 Learning Objectives

- Learners can emphasize important points in their presentations.
- Learners can state the reasons for the importance of certain points.
- Learners can recommend a course of action.

 Warm Up

Work with a partner or in a group. Discuss the following questions.
1. How many items or points should be highlighted during your presentation?
2. What do you normally highlight?
3. Is it always necessary to emphasize something?

Sample Presentation Script

Read the presentation aloud.

> **I want to highlight the importance of our mentorship program.**
>
> Both the mentors and mentees say the program is rewarding. It allows employees to develop better communication skills. It also increases self-confidence and job satisfaction.
>
> **Let me emphasize that our mentors are an integral part of the program.** We need more volunteers to become mentors.

우리 멘토링 프로그램의 중요성을 강조하고 싶습니다.

멘토와 멘티 모두가 이 프로그램이 보람 있다고 합니다. 직원들이 더 원활한 의사소통 능력을 기를 수 있게 해주죠. 또한 자신감과 업무 만족도를 증가시켜 줍니다.

멘토가 이 프로그램의 필수적인 부분이라는 점을 강조합니다. 멘토가 될 수 있는 더 많은 지원자가 필요합니다.

✓ Comprehension Check

Answer the questions.

1. What does the speaker want to highlight?
2. The program increases self-confidence and what else?

Vocabulary

Match the words or expressions with the correct definitions.

1. highlight _____
2. mentee _____
3. rewarding _____
4. allow _____
5. job satisfaction _____
6. integral _____

a. 멘티 (멘토로부터 조언을 받는 사람)
b. 강조하다
c. 업무 만족도
d. 보람 있는
e. 필수적인
f. 가능하게 하다

✓ Vocab Test

Fill in the blanks with the correct words or expressions.

highlight / mentee / rewarding / allows / job satisfaction / integral

1. The program _____ everyone to participate.
2. I have a _____ career.
3. I'd like to _____ this point.
4. An agenda is an _____ part of a meeting.
5. John is the mentor, and Mary is the _____.
6. Their _____ is high.

⊕ Bonus Resources

not just any 일반적인 ~이 아닌

A: What is so special about the client? 그 고객이 뭐가 그리 특별한가요?
B: This is **not just any** client. She is the CEO of Mega, Inc.
이분은 아무 고객이 아닙니다. Mega 사의 CEO이시거든요.

not은 '아닌'를 뜻하고 any는 '아무'를 말하는데, just까지 더하면 '그냥 아무 ~이 아닌'이 된다. 특별한 무엇이나 사람이라는 점을 강조할 때 쓴다.

Grammar Points

Read the following and practice making sentences.

1. I want to highlight ~

> highlight는 특별히 강조하고자 하는 것을 언급할 때 유용한 단어다. I want to highlight ~는 '~을 강조하고 싶습니다'라는 뜻이다. 조금 덜 캐주얼하게는 I would like to를 쓸 수 있다.
>
> *I want to highlight the recent problems.* 최근 문제를 강조하고 싶습니다.

   a) I want to highlight _____ between the two designs.
      두 디자인 간의 차이점을 강조하고 싶습니다.

   b) I want to highlight _____. 주요 쟁점을 강조하고 싶습니다.

   c) I want to highlight _____, not the failures. 실패가 아닌 성공을 강조하고 싶습니다.

2. Let me emphasize that ~

> Let me emphasize that ~은 '~라는 것을 강조합니다'를 뜻한다. that 뒤에는 강조하고 싶은 부분을 주어+동사로 언급하면 된다.
>
> *Let me emphasize that this policy is important.* 이 방침이 중요하다는 점을 강조합니다.

   a) Let me emphasize that _____ agree. 모든 매니저들이 동의한다는 점을 강조합니다.

   b) Let me emphasize that _____ finished. 저희가 끝나지 않았다는 점을 강조합니다.

   c) Let me emphasize that _____ is late. 배송이 지연됐다는 점을 강조합니다.

Practice

Making Sentences

Practice writing sentences. Use the given words or use your own. Then, read your sentences to your partner or group.

1. It allows employees to ~
   (talk freely / take longer vacations / have more freedom)

   - _____
   - _____
   - _____

2. We need more ~
   (ideas / resources / time)

   - _____
   - _____
   - _____

Write

Write a short presentation script that highlights the importance of a document.

_____
_____
_____

Real Presentation

Read the scenario and the four key items on the flashcard. Then, do a portion of a presentation where you highlight the importance of a company program. When another member of your group presents, use the checklist below.

Scenario

> You are an HR executive. You are giving a presentation to your company's managers regarding the annual leadership workshop. You want to highlight its benefits. Most past attendees say the workshop is quite helpful. They can learn about different styles of leadership and get a chance to share ideas. Add that you need more managers for the workshop.

Flashcard

1. annual leadership workshop – helpful	**2.** learn about different styles of leadership
3. a chance to share ideas	**4.** offered only once a year and need more managers

✓ Presentation Checklist	Y	N
The presenter made eye contact with the audience.		
The presenter used gestures and body language.		
The presenter spoke clearly and confidently.		
The presenter correctly used words/expressions from the lesson.		

 **Homework**

You are speaking to a group of people in your company. Write a short part of a presentation where you highlight the importance of a project. Then, record yourself giving the presentation. Listen to your recording and think about how you can improve your presentation.

_____

_____

_____

Warm Up Sample Answers
1. I should highlight (only two / more than two) items or points.
2. I normally highlight (important data / surprising information / the main point).
3. (Yes, it's / No, it's not) always necessary.

Comprehension Check Answers
1. The speaker wants to highlight the importance of their mentorship program.
2. The program also increases job satisfaction.

Vocabulary Answers
1. b, 2. a, 3. d, 4. f, 5. c, 6. e

Vocab Test Answers
1. allows, 2. rewarding, 3. highlight, 4. integral, 5. mentee, 6. job satisfaction

Grammar Points Answers
1. a) the differences b) the main/major issues c) the successes
2. a) all the managers b) we're not c) the shipment

Write Sample Answer
I want to highlight the importance of our project manual.
It allows the project staff to do work efficiently and correctly. It also helps them to reduce errors.

Real Presentation Sample Answer
I want to highlight the benefits of the annual leadership workshop.
Most past attendees say that it's helpful. It allows attendees to learn about different styles of leadership. It also gives them a chance to share ideas.
Let me emphasize that it's offered only once a year. We need more managers to take the workshop.

Homework Sample Answer
I want to highlight the importance of this project.
It's not just any project. It allows us to enter the U.S. market. It also gives us great PR opportunities.
Let me emphasize that your interest in the project is important. We need more support from all of you.

Presentation Tip

On Memorizing or Reading Your Presentation
프레젠테이션을 외우거나 읽는 것에 대하여

Is it okay to memorize or read your presentation? Here are some answers.
프레젠테이션을 외우거나 읽어도 될까? 아래에 몇 가지 답이 있다.

① Memorizing 외우기

Generally, memorizing your presentation is not recommended.
일반적으로 프레젠테이션 외우는 것을 권장하지 않는다.

Reasons: You will most likely sound unnatural. If so, your audience will stop paying attention. What's worse, you might forget what to say. That would be embarrassing for everyone.
이유: 부자연스럽게 들릴 가능성이 높다. 그렇게 되면 청중은 더 이상 집중하지 않을 것이다. 설상가상으로, 해야 할 말을 잊어버릴 수 있다. 그러면 모두에게 난처한 상황이 된다.

Exceptions: You can memorize a minute or two of the beginning. You can also memorize the ending. That can give you confidence. Also, quotations are okay to memorize.
예외: 시작 부분의 1~2분 정도는 외울 수 있다. 마지막 부분도 역시 외울 수 있다. 이는 자신감을 줄 수 있다. 인용문 역시 외워도 좋다.

② Reading 읽기

Reading is also generally not advised. 읽는 것도 일반적으로 권장하지 않는다.

Reasons: You will sound unnatural. Your voice will likely be a monotone. People will feel bored. In addition, you will have little eye contact with the audience. Then, they will focus their attention elsewhere.
이유: 부자연스럽게 들릴 것이다. 목소리는 아마 단조로울 것이다. 사람들은 지루해할 것이다. 게다가 청중과 눈을 자주 마주치지 못할 것이다. 그렇게 되면, 청중은 주위를 다른 곳에 둘 것이다.

Exceptions: Sometimes you might have to read your presentation. Some examples are important documents or speeches. In this case, practice the material enough to interact with the audience.
예외: 때로는 프레젠테이션을 읽어야 할 때가 있다. 예를 들자면, 중요한 문서나 연설이 있다. 이런 경우, 자료를 가지고 충분히 연습하여 청중과 소통하도록 하자.

7 Using Visuals 1

Learning Objectives

- Learners can introduce pictures, charts, or graphs to the audience.
- Learners can explain the meaning of pictures, charts, or graphs.
- Learners can draw conclusions about pictures, charts, or graphs.

Warm Up

Work with a partner or in a group. Discuss the following questions.

1. Do you use many pictures in your presentation?
2. How many charts or graphs do you usually use during a presentation?
3. What is your favorite color to use for charts or graphs?

Sample Presentation Script

Read the presentation aloud.

On the left, you can see a photo of the most recent group of interns. They all look really happy and enthusiastic, don't they?

Okay, let's now look at some significant figures from the last five years.

In this chart, the vertical axis represents the total number of participants. Here, we see a steady increase year after year.

왼쪽에 저희 가장 최근 인턴들의 사진을 보실 수 있습니다. 정말 즐겁고 열정이 넘쳐 보이죠, 그렇죠?

자, 이제 지난 5년간 몇 가지 중요한 수치를 함께 보겠습니다.

이 차트에서 세로축은 전체 참가자 수를 보여주고 있습니다. 여기서, 참가자 수가 해마다 꾸준히 증가하는 것을 보실 수 있습니다.

✓ Comprehension Check

Answer the questions.

1. What can the audience see on the left?
2. What does the vertical axis represent in the chart?

Vocabulary

Match the words or expressions with the correct definitions.

1. most recent _____
2. enthusiastic _____
3. significant _____
4. figures _____
5. total number _____
6. year after year _____

a. 수치, 숫자
b. 가장 최근
c. 전체 수, 총계
d. 매년
e. 열광적인
f. 의미 있는, 중요한

✓ Vocab Test

Fill in the blanks with the correct words or expressions.

most recent / enthusiastic / significant / figures / total number / year after year

1. These are last year's sales _____.
2. Let me see the _____ report.
3. The crowd is really _____.
4. We did well _____.
5. That's a _____ change from last year.
6. What is the _____ of attendees?

⊕ Bonus Resources

a spike 급등, 급증

A: Wow, there was **a spike** in sales in December. 와, 12월에 매출이 급등했네요.
B: It was probably due to the holiday season. 아마 연말 휴가철 때문이었을 겁니다.

spike는 못 같은 뾰족한 것을 뜻하는데, 비격식적인 표현으로 가격이나 수치가 갑자기 빠르게 오르는 현상을 의미하기도 한다. 흔히 뒤에 in과 함께 급증한 그 '무엇'을 언급하기도 한다.

Grammar Points

Read the following and practice making sentences.

1. On the left/right, you can see ~

> On the left/right, you can see ~는 '왼쪽/오른쪽에 ~을 보실 수 있습니다'를 말한다. 흔히 슬라이드에서 위치를 가리키면서 쓰는데, 청중이 주목해야 할 요소를 언급할 때 매우 유용하다.
>
> *On the left, you can see a pie chart.* 왼쪽에 원그래프를 보실 수 있습니다.

a) On the right, you can see _____. 오른쪽에 그 두 가지 색상을 보실 수 있습니다.

b) On the left, you can see _____. 왼쪽에 흑백사진 하나를 보실 수 있습니다.

c) On the left, you can see _____. 왼쪽에 동그라미를 보실 수 있습니다.

2. The horizontal/vertical axis represents ~

> The horizontal/vertical axis represents ~는 '이 차트에서 수평축/세로축은 ~을 보여줍니다'를 말한다. horizontal axis 대신 x-axis, 그리고 vertical axis 대신 y-axis라는 표현을 쓰기도 한다.
>
> *The horizontal axis represents the years.* 이 차트에서 수평축은 연도를 보여줍니다.

a) The horizontal axis represents _____. 이 차트에서 가로축은 시간을 보여줍니다.

b) The vertical axis represents _____. 이 차트에서 세로축은 평균 가격을 보여줍니다.

c) In this chart, the vertical axis represents _____.

   이 차트에서 세로축은 가계 소득을 보여줍니다.

 **Practice**

Making Sentences

Practice writing sentences. Use the given words or use your own. Then, read your sentences to your partner or group.

1. They all look ~
   (interested / very tired / young)

   - _____
   - _____
   - _____

2. Here, we see ~
   (another photo / that chart / the new logo)

   - _____
   - _____
   - _____

Write

Write a short presentation script that describes a photo, drawing, or chart on the left or right side (of a slide).

_____
_____
_____

Real Presentation

Read the scenario and the four key items on the flashcard. Then, do a portion of a presentation where you talk about a new public works project. When another member of your group presents, use the checklist below.

Scenario

> You are an engineer from a civil engineering firm. You are giving a presentation to some government workers. You're talking about a new bridge for the city. You're showing a color sketch and a graph showing the anticipated traffic on the new bridge for the next ten years. The total number of cars are indicated on the vertical axis. It is expected that they will see a steady increase in traffic year after year.

Flashcard

1. a color sketch of the new bridge	**2.** next, look at the anticipated traffic
3. vertical axis – the total number of cars	**4.** a steady increase in traffic year after year

✓ Presentation Checklist	Y	N
The presenter made eye contact with the audience.		
The presenter used gestures and body language.		
The presenter spoke clearly and confidently.		
The presenter correctly used words/expressions from the lesson.		

Homework

You are speaking to a group of managers in your company. Write a short part of a presentation where you describe the sales results of a new product. Then, record yourself giving the presentation. Listen to your recording and think about how you can improve your presentation.

Warm Up Sample Answers
1. (Yes, I / No, I don't) use many pictures.
2. I usually use (only one or two / two to four / many) charts or graphs.
3. My favorite color for charts or graphs is (green/blue/black).

Comprehension Check Answers
1. The audience can see a photo of the most recent group of interns.
2. The vertical axis represents the total number of participants.

Vocabulary Answers
1. b, 2. e, 3. f, 4. a, 5. c, 6. d

Vocab Test Answers
1. figures, 2. most recent, 3. enthusiastic, 4. year after year, 5. significant, 6. total number

Grammar Points Answers
1. a) the two colors b) a black-and-white picture c) a circle
2. a) the time/duration b) the average price c) the household income

Write Sample Answer
On the right, you can see the two new design ideas. They both look pretty nice, don't they? I really like them both.

Real Presentation Sample Answer
On the right, you can see a color sketch of the new bridge. It looks really state-of-the art, doesn't it?
Okay, let's now look at the anticipated traffic on the new bridge over the next ten years.
In this graph, the vertical axis represents the total number of cars. Here, we see a steady increase in traffic year after year.

Homework Sample Answer
On the left, you can see a photo of our newest PC tablet, TabGo. It looks really slim and light, doesn't it?
Okay, let's look at some important sales figures from the last six months.
In this chart, the vertical axis represents the total monthly revenue. Here, we see a spike in sales in March.

Presentation Tip

Choosing the Right Visuals for Your Presentation
프레젠테이션에 맞는 비주얼을 선택하기

Let's look at some of the possible visual aids you can use. What should you use? It will depend on the subject, presentation length, and the audience.
사용할 수 있는 몇 가지 비주얼 도구를 함께 보자. 무엇을 사용해야 할까? 주제, 프레젠테이션 길이, 청중에 따라 다르다.

① Slides 슬라이드

Slide software such as PowerPoint is relatively easy to use. Slides can be created and revised easily. These slides can also be used during online meetings. However, skipping to a particular slide is not easy.
파워포인트 같은 슬라이드 소프트웨어는 비교적 사용하기가 쉽다. 슬라이드를 만들고 쉽게 수정할 수 있다. 이런 슬라이드는 온라인 미팅에서도 사용할 수도 있다. 그러나 특정 슬라이드로 이동하기가 쉽지 않다.

② Prezi 프레지

Prezi is more flexible than PowerPoint. It has a non-linear approach with a zooming effect. Unfortunately, Prezi can only be used when you're online.
프레지는 파워포인트보다 더 유연적이다. 줌 효과가 있는 비선형 접근 방식을 사용한다. 아쉽게도 온라인 경우에만 사용할 수 있다.

③ Flipchart 플립 차트

Flipcharts are easy to use while moving around. They are good for brainstorming and team sessions. You can write and draw on the flipchart as you speak.
플립 차트는 이동하면서 사용하기에 수월하나. 브레인스토밍과 팀 회의 때 유용하나. 말하면서 무언가를 쓰거나 그릴 수 있다.

④ Whiteboard 화이트보드

Whiteboards are good to use for small groups. You can write or draw as you speak. If you use a digital whiteboard, you can save and print what you write.
화이트보드는 소수 그룹에서 사용하기 좋다. 말하면서 쓰고 그릴 수 있다. 디지털 화이트보드를 쓰면 내용을 저장하고 출력도 할 수 있다.

8 Using Visuals 2

Learning Objectives

- **Learners can draw attention to a video clip.**
- **Learners can explain what is happening in a video clip.**
- **Learners can present an article and describe what's in it.**

Warm Up

Work with a partner or in a group. Discuss the following questions.

1. Are videos effective in presentations?
2. How long should a video be in a presentation?
3. Do you often use an article in your presentation?

Sample Presentation Script

Read the presentation aloud.

> **This is a clip of one of our focus groups discussing our products.**
>
> Let's watch it for a minute.
>
> It was a great group, right? Everyone gave great productive feedback, and we heard them.
>
> **If you take a look at this article, you'll notice our customer satisfaction scores.**
> As you can see, they are quite high.

이것은 우리 제품에 대해서 논의하는 포커스 그룹 중 하나를 담은 영상입니다.

잠깐 보시죠.

훌륭한 그룹 아닌가요? 모두 아주 생산적인 피드백을 주셨고, 저희는 귀담아들었죠.

이 기사를 보시면, 저희 고객 만족 점수가 눈에 들어오실 겁니다.
보시다시피, 꽤 높습니다.

✓ Comprehension Check

Answer the questions.

1. What is the focus group discussing in the clip?
2. What does the speaker say are quite high?

Vocabulary

Match the words or expressions with the correct definitions.

1. focus group _____
2. productive _____
3. feedback _____
4. notice _____
5. score _____
6. quite _____

a. 피드백, 조언
b. 주목하다, 인지하다
c. 점수
d. 생산적인
e. 꽤, 상당히
f. 포커스 그룹, 소비자 그룹

✓ Vocab Test

Fill in the blanks with the correct words or expressions.

focus group / productive / feedback / notice / score / quite

1. The _____ liked the old model better.
2. What was your evaluation _____?
3. Do you _____ any difference?
4. Your presentation was _____ good.
5. It was a _____ meeting.
6. I need your honest _____.

⊕ Bonus Resources

run it back (특정 목적을 위해) ~을 다시 하다

A: Did you catch the CEO in the video? 영상에서 CEO 보셨어요?
B: I'm not sure. Can you **run it back**? 잘 모르겠어요. 다시 보여 주시겠어요?

run back은 원래 어딘가로 급히 돌아가는 것을 의미한다. 비격식적인 표현으로 영상이나 음악을 다시 재생하는 것 역시 run back한다고 한다.

# Grammar Points

Read the following and practice making sentences.

1. **This is a clip of ~**

> This is a clip of ~는 '이것은 ~을 찍은 영상입니다'라는 뜻이다. This is가 들어가는 아주 기본적인 표현으로, clip 대신 video라고 해도 무방하다.
>
> 📖 *This is a clip of* the event. 이것은 그 행사를 찍은 영상입니다.

   a) This is a clip of _____. 이것은 컨퍼런스를 찍은 영상입니다.

   b) This is a clip of _____. 이것은 저희 이사님 중 한 분을 찍은 영상입니다.

   c) This is a clip of _____ to the meeting.
      이것은 저희가 회의로 걸어가는 것을 찍은 영상입니다.

2. **If you take a look at this article, you'll ~**

> If you는 '당신이 ~하면'을, take a look을 무언가를 '한번 보다'를 뜻한다. If you take a look at this article, you'll ~은 '이 기사를 보시면, ~하실 겁니다'라는 것을 말한다.
>
> 📖 *If you take a look at this article, you'll* see what I mean.
> 이 기사를 보시면, 제 말이 무슨 뜻인지 아실 겁니다.

   a) If you take a look at this article, you'll _____ why.
      이 기사를 보시면, 그 이유를 이해하실 겁니다.

   b) If you take a look at this article, you'll _____. 이 기사를 보시면, 이름들이 보이실 겁니다.

   c) If you take a look at this article, you'll _____. 이 기사를 보시면, 놀라실 겁니다.

 **Practice**

Making Sentences

Practice writing sentences. Use the given words or use your own. Then, read your sentences to your partner or group.

1. Let's watch it ~
   (now / later / for a few minutes)

   - _____
   - _____
   - _____

2. As you can see, ~
   (it's a nice photo / it's big / they are amazing)

   - _____
   - _____
   - _____

Write

Write a short presentation script that introduces and briefly describes a clip.

_____
_____
_____

 **Real Presentation**

Read the scenario and the four key items on the flashcard. Then, do a portion of a presentation where you talk about a fundraising event. When another member of your group presents, use the checklist below.

Scenario

> You are a public relations executive at a large corporation. You're addressing other executives regarding a fundraiser you had in July. You'll first show a clip. There was a big turnout, and you raised a lot of money. Then you'll tell the audience to look at an article that shows the final amount. It's over a million dollars.

Flashcard

1. clip – fundraiser in July	**2.** enjoyed the event & raised a lot of money
3. article – final amount	**4.** over a million dollars

✓ Presentation Checklist	Y	N
The presenter made eye contact with the audience.		
The presenter used gestures and body language.		
The presenter spoke clearly and confidently.		
The presenter correctly used words/expressions from the lesson.		

Homework

You are speaking to an internal group of executives. Write a short part of a presentation where you describe an incident at one of the company's stores. Then, record yourself giving the presentation. Listen to your recording and think about how you can improve your presentation.

___

___

___

Warm Up Sample Answers
1. (Yes, they are / No, they are not) effective.
2. It should be (very short / less than five minutes long / about five to ten minutes long).
3. (Yes, I / No, I don't) often use an article in my presentation.

Comprehension Check Answers
1. The group is discussing the company's products.
2. The speaker says the customer satisfaction scores are quite high.

Vocabulary Answers
1. f, 2. d, 3. a, 4. b, 5. c, 6. e

Vocab Test Answers
1. focus group, 2. score, 3. notice, 4. quite, 5. productive, 6. feedback

Grammar Points Answers
1. a) the conference b) one of our directors c) us walking
2. a) understand b) see the names c) be surprised

Write Sample Answer
This is a clip of one of our factory tours last year.
It was a large group, right? Everyone had a chance to see how our products are made.

Real Presentation Sample Answer
This is a clip of our fundraiser in July.
Let's watch it now.
It was big turnout, right? Everyone really enjoyed the event, and we raised a lot of money.
If you take a look at this article, you'll see the final amount.
As you can see, it's over a million dollars.

Homework Sample Answer
This is a clip of the small fire that occurred in the store.
Let's watch it now.
It was a little too fast, right? Let me run it back. Our staff got all the customers out safely, and everyone was safe.
If you take a look at this article, you'll notice that the fire was put out quickly.
As you can see, it was just a minor incident.

> **Presentation Tip**

Creating Visually Accessible Presentation Slides
시각적으로 이해하기 쉬운 프레젠테이션 슬라이드 만들기

Good presentation slides have the following characteristics. Think of the following as a checklist.
좋은 슬라이드는 다음과 같은 특징이 있다. 다음을 체크리스트로 고민해 보자.

① **Legible** 글자가 잘 보이는가?

All fonts are large enough. Ask yourself: can the words be read from all the way in the back? Do they stand out from the background?
모든 폰트가 충분히 크다. 스스로에게 질문해 보자: 맨 뒷자리에서도 글자를 읽을 수 있는가? 배경과 구별되는가?

② **Necessary** 꼭 필요한가?

Anything that is unnecessary is deleted. This includes graphics or even slides.
어떤 것이라도 필요 없는 것은 삭제한다. 도표나 슬라이드조차도 마찬가지다.

③ **Uniform** 일관성이 있는가?

The design, colors, and fonts are consistent. Each slide looks like it belongs to the whole.
디자인과 색깔, 폰트가 일관되어 있다. 각 슬라이드가 마치 전체 슬라이드에 속한 것처럼 보인다.

④ **Comprehensible** 이해하기 쉬운가?

The audience can understand the slide immediately. The text and graphics are easy to understand.
청중이 슬라이드를 바로 이해할 수 있다. 본문과 그래픽을 쉽게 파악할 수 있다.

⑤ **Focused** 내용이 집중적으로 잘 들어가 있는가?

Only one idea is included in each slide. Otherwise, the audience will be confused. Also, everything in a slide supports the main point.
슬라이드마다 딱 한 가지 아이디어가 존재한다. 그렇지 않으면 청중이 혼란스러워할 것이다. 또한 슬라이드에 담긴 모든 요소는 요점을 뒷받침한다.

⑥ **Functioning** 제대로 작동되는가?

The slides flow as you've intended. Each special effect or animation works.
슬라이드가 내가 의도한 대로 흘러간다. 특수 효과와 애니메이션 모두 잘 작동한다.

9 Expressing Opinions and Recommendations

 Learning Objectives

- Learners can express opinions during presentations.
- Learners can offer recommendations during presentations.
- Learners can give reasons for making a recommendation.

 Warm Up

Work with a partner or in a group. Discuss the following questions.

1. Do you often express opinions during presentations?
2. Are you good at making recommendations?
3. During a presentation, when should you make recommendations?

Sample Presentation Script

Read the presentation aloud.

So far, I've discussed the benefits of adopting cloud-based solutions.

So, what are the downsides? You know, I can't think of one.
Avery Corp. is offering us a substantial discount. It really is a good offer.

In my view, we should move forward and switch to this platform.
I strongly recommend taking a closer look at the brochure. You'll discover even more benefits that come with this platform.

지금까지 클라우드 기반 설루션 도입의 혜택에 대해 말씀드렸습니다.

그럼, 단점은 뭐가 있을까요? 그게 말이죠, 하나도 떠오르지 않습니다.
Avery 사가 저희에게 큰 폭의 할인을 해주겠다고 합니다. 정말 좋은 제안입니다.

저희가 앞으로 나아가서 이 플랫폼으로 전환해야 한다고 생각합니다.
브로슈어를 자세히 살펴보기를 강력히 추천합니다. 이 플랫폼이 제공하는 더 많은 혜택을 확인하실 수 있습니다.

✓ Comprehension Check

Answer the questions.

1. What has the speaker discussed so far?
2. What is Avery Corp. offering?

Vocabulary

Match the words or expressions with the correct definitions.

1. benefit _____
2. adopt _____
3. downside _____
4. substantial _____
5. discount _____
6. strongly recommend _____

a. 부정적인 면, 단점
b. 할인
c. 큰 폭의, 상당한
d. 도입하다
e. 강력히 추천하다
f. 혜택, 이득

✓ Vocab Test

Fill in the blanks with the correct words or expressions.

benefits / adopt / downside / substantial / discount / strongly recommend

1. I'm getting a _____ raise.
2. Let's _____ this new technology.
3. What are the _____?
4. There is an upside and a _____.
5. They gave us a _____.
6. I _____ eating at the cafeteria.

⊕ Bonus Resources

on the fence 고민 중인, 결정하지 못하는

A: So, are you going to call Tom? 그래서 Tom에게 전화할 건가요?
B: I'm still **on the fence**. Maybe I'll just email him.
   아직 고민 중입니다. 그냥 그분에게 이메일을 보낼까 봐요.

on the fence는 직역으로 '울타리 위에'다. 결정을 하지 않은 채 울타리 위에 앉아 양쪽 다 보고만 있는 것에 비유해서 생긴 말이다.

Grammar Points

Read the following and practice making sentences.

1. In my view, we should ~

> In my view는 '제 생각에는'이란 뜻이다. 그리고 we should는 '우리는 ~을 해야 한다'로, 뒤에 해야 하는 것을 동사로 언급하면 된다.
>
> *In my view, we should take their offer.* 제 생각에는 그들의 제안을 수용해야 합니다.

a) In my view, we should _____ it. 제 생각에는 그걸 다시 고려해야 합니다.
b) In my view, we should _____. 제 생각에는 Mary와 함께 일해야 합니다.
c) In my view, we should _____ the project. 제 생각에는 프로젝트를 늦춰야 합니다.

2. I strongly recommend + ~ing

> I recommend + ~ing는 '~할 것을 추천합니다'라는 뜻이다. recommend 앞에 '강력히'를 의미하는 strongly를 붙이면서 '~할 것을 강력히 추천합니다'가 된다.
>
> *I strongly recommend moving the date.* 날짜를 변경할 것을 강력히 추천합니다.

a) I strongly recommend _____ for advice. John에게 조언을 구할 것을 강력히 추천합니다.
b) I strongly recommend _____ to their office. 그쪽 사무실로 갈 것을 강력히 추천합니다.
c) I strongly recommend _____ to them. 그들과 대화할 것을 강력히 추천합니다.

Practice

Making Sentences

Practice writing sentences. Use the given words or use your own. Then, read your sentences to your partner or group.

1. I've discussed ~
   (the problem / the pros and cons / the project's progress)

   - _____
   - _____
   - _____

2. It really is ~
   (a good product / a nice gesture / a bad idea)

   - _____
   - _____
   - _____

Write

Write a short presentation script that briefly expresses an opinion and makes a recommendation.

_____
_____
_____

Real Presentation

Read the scenario and the four key items on the flashcard. Then, offer an opinion and make a recommendation to the audience. When another member of your group presents, use the checklist below.

Scenario

You are a purchasing manager. You're talking to some decision-makers in the company regarding two maintenance proposals. The one proposed by AAA Corp. is offering a better price. You think your company should go with it. You then make a recommendation to start negotiations with the AAA Corp.

Flashcard

1. two maintenance proposals	**2.** AAA Corp. - better price & good proposal
3. should go with the offer	**4.** recommend starting negotiations with AAA Corp.

✓ Presentation Checklist	Y	N
The presenter made eye contact with the audience.		
The presenter used gestures and body language.		
The presenter spoke clearly and confidently.		
The presenter correctly used words/expressions from the lesson.		

Homework

You are speaking to the executives in your company. Write a short ending of a presentation where you express your opinion and make a recommendation on a new office. Then, record yourself giving the presentation. Listen to your recording and think about how you can improve your presentation.

Warm Up Sample Answers
1. (Yes, I / No, I don't) often express opinions during presentations.
2. (Yes, I'm / No, I'm not) good at making recommendations.
3. You should make recommendations (after the summary / anytime / in the middle).

Comprehension Check Answers
1. The speaker has discussed the benefits of adopting cloud-based solutions.
2. Avery Corp. is offering a substantial discount.

Vocabulary Answers
1. f, 2. d, 3. a, 4. c, 5. b, 6. e

Vocab Test Answers
1. substantial, 2. adopt, 3. benefits, 4. downside, 5. discount, 6. strongly recommend

Grammar Points Answers
1. a) reconsider b) work with Mary c) delay
2. a) asking John b) going c) talking

Write Sample Answer
In my view, we should redesign the logo for the product.
I strongly recommend adding some colors to it.

Real Presentation Sample Answer
I've discussed the two maintenance proposals in detail.
So, which is better? The answer is simple.
AAA Corp. is offering us a better price. It really is a good proposal.
In my view, we should go with them.
I strongly recommend starting negotiations with AAA Corp.

Homework Sample Answer
I've discussed all the benefits of opening an office in San Francisco.
So, what is the downside? It'll cost money, of course.
That's why many of you are still on the fence. It really is something to think about.
In my view, we should open the office.
I strongly recommend starting small at first.

Presentation Tip

An Effective Way to Present a Recommendation
효율적으로 건의하는 방법

Sometimes the audience needs more convincing. Here is one effective way to present your recommendation.
때로는 청중을 더 설득할 필요가 있다. 효율적으로 건의하는 방법 하나를 소개한다.

① What is 현 상황

Start by presenting the current situation very clearly. The members of your audience need to have a clear picture in their minds.
현 상황을 명확하게 보여주는 것으로 시작한다. 청중의 머릿속에 선명하게 그려져야 한다.

> *Feedback indicates our customer service response times are too long.*
> 고객 서비스 응답 시간이 너무 길다는 피드백이 있습니다.
> *As we stand today, our operational efficiency is not meeting our projected targets.*
> 현재로서는 운영 효율성이 예상 목표에 미치지 못하고 있습니다.

② What you would do 나라면?

If you say "you" immediately, the audience might get defensive. Instead, say what you would do. They are free not to follow your example.
만약 바로 '당신들'이라고 하면, 청중은 방어적인 태도를 취할 수 있다. 대신 나라면 어떻게 하겠다는 것을 말한다. 나의 방식을 따를 필요는 없다.

> *I would want to restructure our customer service.* 저라면 고객 서비스를 재구성하고 싶습니다.
> *If I were to address this issue, I would first conduct a comprehensive market analysis.*
> 제가 이 문제를 해결하고자 한다면, 가장 먼저 종합적인 시장 분석할 것입니다.

③ What could be 미래

Let them see why they should follow your recommendation. Show them that what you suggest is possible.
나의 건의를 따라야 하는 이유를 알려준다. 내가 제안하는 것이 가능하다는 것을 보여주자.

> *Exploring flexible work solutions could boost productivity.*
> 유연한 근무 솔루션을 모색하면 생산성을 향상할 수 있을 것입니다.
> *One solution could be to embrace a more flexible project management style.*
> 하나의 해결책은 유연한 프로젝트 관리 스타일을 수용하는 것입니다.

10 Summarizing Key Points

 Learning Objectives

- Learners can signal the end of the main body of a presentation.
- Learners can summarize the main points of a presentation.
- Learners can offer a conclusion as needed.

 Warm Up

Work with a partner or in a group. Discuss the following questions.

1. Why is summarizing important at the end of a presentation?
2. When is it unnecessary to summarize the main points?
3. Should you include new information during the summary?

Sample Presentation Script

Read the presentation aloud.

That covers everything.

Let's briefly recap what the program offers.

First, it gives the interns a chance to learn real skills related to their chosen fields. It also allows them to get feedback from seasoned managers.

Finally, it lets them figure out what their strong points are.

In short, the internship is a great opportunity for recent graduates.

이것으로 모든 것을 다루었습니다.

이 프로그램이 제공하는 것을 간단히 정리해 보죠.

우선, 인턴들에게 자신이 선택한 분야와 관련된 실제 기술을 배울 기회를 줍니다. 또한 경험 많은 관리자들로부터 피드백을 받을 수 있게 해줍니다.

마지막으로, 본인들의 장점이 무엇인지 알아내게 해줍니다.

간단히 말하자면, 이 인턴십 제도는 최근에 졸업한 학생들에게 아주 좋은 기회입니다.

✓ Comprehension Check

Answer the questions.

1. What skills do interns get a chance to learn?
2. The internship is a great opportunity for whom?

 **Vocabulary**

Match the words or expressions with the correct definitions.

1. recap _____
2. related to _____
3. chosen _____
4. seasoned _____
5. figure out _____
6. recent _____

a. 정리하다, 개요를 말하다
b. 최근의
c. 선택된
d. ~와 관련된
e. 알아내다
f. 노련한, 경험 많은

✓ Vocab Test

Fill in the blanks with the correct words or expressions.

recap / related to / chosen / seasoned / figure out / recent

1. The CEO is the board's _____ leader.
2. Let's _____ what happened.
3. _____ what the problem is.
4. These documents are _____ the project.
5. The _____ strike delayed our shipment.
6. She is a _____ professional.

⊕ Bonus Resources

breathing room 숨 돌릴 기회, 생각할 여유

A: The deadline has been extended. 마감 시한이 연장되었습니다.
B: Great! That gives us some **breathing room**. 좋네요! 숨 좀 쉴 수 있겠네요.

여기서 room은 space와 유사한 '공간'을 뜻한다. '숨을 쉬는'을 뜻하는 breathing이 앞에 붙으면서 '숨을 쉬는 공간'이라고 직역된다. 여유를 의미하는 것이다.

 **Grammar Points**

Read the following and practice making sentences.

1. Let's briefly recap ~

> Let's는 Let us의 줄임말로, 함께 무언가를 하자를 의미한다. '간단히'의 뜻을 가진 briefly와 함께 '다시 정리하다'를 말하는 recap을 함께 쓰면 '~을 간단히 정리해 보겠습니다'가 된다.
>
> Ex *Let's briefly recap* what we've discussed. 저희가 논의한 것을 간단히 정리해 보겠습니다.

a) Let's briefly recap _____. 모든 것을 간단히 정리해 보겠습니다.

b) Let's briefly recap what _____. 당신이 말한 것을 간단히 정리해 보겠습니다.

c) Let's briefly recap _____. 쟁점을 간단히 정리해 보겠습니다.

2. In short, ~

> In short, ~는 '간단히 말하자면', '한마디로 말하자면'이라는 뜻으로, 뒤에 현재 다루고 있는 쟁점이나 결론의 핵심을 주어+동사로 짧게 언급하면 된다.
>
> Ex *In short*, we need more staff. 간단히 말하자면, 저희는 더 많은 직원이 필요합니다.

a) In short, _____ upset. 간단히 말하자면, 고객이 화가 나 있습니다.

b) In short, _____ a great program. 간단히 말하자면, 이것은 좋은 프로그램입니다.

c) In short, _____ resolved. 간단히 말하자면, 문제는 해결됐습니다.

 **Practice**

Making Sentences

Practice writing sentences. Use the given words or use your own. Then, read your sentences to your partner or group.

1. That covers ~

   (all the points / the sales results / today's topic)

   - _____
   - _____
   - _____

2. It lets them ~

   (relax more / work better / leave earlier)

   - _____
   - _____
   - _____

Write

Write a short presentation script that briefly recaps a short, internal presentation.

_____
_____
_____

Real Presentation

Read the scenario and the four key items on the flashcard. Then, do a portion of a presentation where you recap its main points. When another member of your group presents, use the checklist below.

Scenario

> You are an executive for an electronics company. You're making a presentation to a general audience regarding a new product. Your company has just launched the Model IC. Before closing, you're recapping its new features. It comes in three different sizes and allows users to customize the key settings and add great apps for free. You want to highlight that it is the best model developed so far.

Flashcard

1. Model IC	**2.** recap: comes in three different sizes
3. - can customize the key settings - can add great apps for free	**4.** the best model

✓ Presentation Checklist	Y	N
The presenter made eye contact with the audience.		
The presenter used gestures and body language.		
The presenter spoke clearly and confidently.		
The presenter correctly used words/expressions from the lesson.		

Homework

You are speaking to your team members. Write a short part a presentation where you recap some changes in a contract. Then, record yourself giving the presentation. Listen to your recording and think about how you can improve your presentation.

Warm Up Sample Answers
1. It's important because it (helps the audience remember the main points / reinforces the message).
2. It's unnecessary (for very short presentations / during internal meetings).
3. (Yes, you should / No, you shouldn't) include new information.

Comprehension Check Answers
1. They get a chance to learn real skills related to their chosen fields.
2. It's a great opportunity for recent graduates.

Vocabulary Answers
1. a, 2. d, 3. c, 4. f, 5. e, 6. b

Vocab Test Answers
1. chosen, 2. recap, 3. Figure out, 4. related to, 5. recent, 6. seasoned

Grammar Points Answers
1. a) everything b) you said c) the issues
2. a) the client is b) this is c) the problem is

Write Sample Answer
Let's briefly recap what we know about the project so far.
First, the project is in Chicago. It's also a very large project.
Finally, it will start early this year.

Real Presentation Sample Answer
That covers Model IC.
Let's briefly recap its new features.
First, it comes in three different sizes. It also allows users to customize the key settings.
Finally, it lets them add great apps for free.
In short, this is the best model we've developed so far.

Homework Sample Answer
That covers everything.
Let's briefly recap the main changes in the revised contract.
First, it gives us more time to finish the two projects. It also allows us to alter the landscaping.
Finally, it lets us use the owner's warehouse.
In short, the revised contract gives us some breathing room.

Presentation Tip

How to Give an Effective Summary
효율적으로 요약하는 방법

① **Refer back to your objectives.** 목표를 다시 언급한다.

You stated your objectives at the beginning of your presentation. Remind your audience of those objectives. Show how the content of your presentation has addressed these goals.

프레젠테이션 도입부에서 목표를 언급했다. 청중에게 이 목표를 다시 한번 알려주자. 프레젠테이션 내용이 어떤 식으로 그 목표를 충족시켰는지 보여준다.

② **Keep it concise.** 간단하게 요약한다.

A summary should be brief and to the point. Avoid going into too much detail. What if you've covered a complex topic? Even then, make sure to use simple language.

요약은 짧고 간단명료해야 한다. 너무 많은 디테일을 말하는 것을 피하자. 복잡한 주제를 다루었다면? 그렇더라도 반드시 쉬운 언어를 사용한다.

③ **Use repetition.** 아이디어를 다시 언급한다.

Repeating key phrases or concepts can be effective in a summary. This is because it reinforces important points. However, be cautious not to overdo it.

요약에서 핵심 표현과 아이디어를 거듭 언급하는 것이 효과적일 수 있다. 주요 쟁점을 강조할 수 있기 때문이다. 그러나 과도하게 하는 것은 피하자.

④ **Avoid adding new information as much as possible.**
가능한 한 새로운 정보를 추가하지 않는다.

Think about why you are giving a summary of your presentation. The summary is meant to reinforce the key points you've already made. Of course, you might have additional information. If so, consider sharing it during the Q&A session.

왜 프레젠테이션을 요약하는지 생각해 보자. 요약은 내가 이미 언급한 주요 쟁점을 강조하기 위해서 하는 것이다. 물론 추가 정보를 공유하고 싶을 수 있다. 이럴 때는 Q&A 시간 때 다룰 것을 고려하자.

11 Closing

Learning Objectives

- Learners can close a presentation with appropriate expressions.
- Learners can express their hope that the presentation was useful.
- Learners can thank the audience for coming.

Warm Up

Work with a partner or in a group. Discuss the following questions.

1. How important is the closing part of the presentation?
2. Are your closings generally short or long?
3. Do you think your closings are usually strong?

Sample Presentation Script

Read the presentation aloud.

> **I hope the presentation was helpful to you.**
>
> I know many of you have been curious about the new privacy policy. Perhaps now you've gained some understanding of the policy.
>
> For those wanting more information, my contact information is on the whiteboard.
>
> **It's been a pleasure presenting to you all.**
>
> Again, thank you.

이 프레젠테이션이 여러분에게 도움이 되었기를 바랍니다.

많은 분이 개인정보 보호 방침에 대해서 궁금해하신 것으로 알고 있습니다. 아마 이제 이 방침에 대해 이해가 좀 됐을 겁니다.

더 많은 정보를 원하시는 분들을 위해, 제 연락처는 화이트보드에 적혀 있습니다.

여러분 모두에게 발표하게 된 것을 기쁘게 생각합니다.

다시 한번 감사드립니다.

✓ Comprehension Check

Answer the questions.

1. What type of policy was the speaker talking about?
2. Where is the speaker's contact information?

Vocabulary

Match the words or expressions with the correct definitions.

1. helpful _____
2. curious _____
3. policy _____
4. gain _____
5. those _____
6. contact information _____

a. ~하게 되다, 얻다
b. 도움이 되는
c. 궁금한
d. 사람들
e. 방침
f. 연락처

✓ Vocab Test

Fill in the blanks with the correct words or expressions.

helpful / curious / policy / gain / those / contact information

1. That was really _____.
2. This is the overtime _____.
3. I'm _____ about the new product.
4. I have to _____ more experience.
5. I need your _____.
6. _____ needing assistance can talk to me.

⊕ Bonus Resources

wrap up 마무리 짓다

A: Uh, Kevin? It's almost noon. 아, Kevin? 거의 12시인데요.
B: Already? Okay. Let's **wrap up** the meeting. 벌써요? 그래요. 회의를 마무리하죠.

wrap은 '포장하다', '싸다', up은 '완전히, 다'로 wrap up은 '싸버리다'라는 뜻이다. 이를 비유해서 무언가를 끝낸다고 할 때 사용한다.

 **Grammar Points**

Read the following and practice making sentences.

1. I hope the presentation was ~

> I hope는 '나는 기대한다', '나는 바란다'라는 뜻으로, I hope this presentation was ~는 '이 프레젠테이션이 ~이었기를 바랍니다'가 된다. 뒤에는 다양한 형용사를 붙일 수 있다.
>
> *I hope the presentation was enlightening.* 이 프레젠테이션이 이해에 도움이 되었기를 바랍니다.

a) I hope the presentation was _____. 이 프레젠테이션이 유익하였기를 바랍니다.

b) I hope the presentation was _____. 이 프레젠테이션이 즐거웠기를 바랍니다.

c) I hope the presentation was _____. 이 프레젠테이션이 도움이 되었기를 바랍니다.

2. It's been a pleasure + ~ing

> It's been a pleasure + ~ing는 '~하게 된 것을 기쁘게 생각합니다'라는 의미가 있다. 상대방과 함께한 어떤 일에 대해 비교적 격식을 차려 긍정적인 언급을 하는 것이다.
>
> *It's been a pleasure talking to you.* 얘기를 나누게 된 것을 기쁘게 생각합니다.

a) It's been a pleasure _____ with everyone. 모두와 함께 일하게 된 것을 기쁘게 생각합니다.

b) It's been a pleasure _____ with you. 당신과 만나게 된 것을 기쁘게 생각합니다.

c) It's been a pleasure _____ with your team.
그쪽 팀과 비즈니스를 하게 된 것을 기쁘게 생각합니다.

 **Practice**

Making Sentences

Practice writing sentences. Use the given words or use your own. Then, read your sentences to your partner or group.

1. I know many of you ~
   (wanted to talk / knew about this / have seen it)

   • _____
   • _____
   • _____

2. Perhaps now you ~
   (have learned something / know the reasons / understand why)

   • _____
   • _____
   • _____

Write

Write a short presentation script that briefly states that you hope your presentation was helpful.

_____
_____
_____

Real Presentation

Read the scenario and the four key items on the flashcard. Then, do the ending portion of a presentation. When another member of your group presents, use the checklist below.

Scenario

> You are the training manager at the HR Division. You're now at the end of the presentation. You're talking to an interested group of employees regarding this year's training programs. You believe that they now have a better idea of what the programs offer. Express hope that the presentation was useful and thank the audience. Also, tell them to contact you if they want more information.

Flashcard

1. curious about this year's training programs	2. have a good idea what's being offered
3. email or call for more information	4. pleasure talking about the programs

✓ Presentation Checklist	Y	N
The presenter made eye contact with the audience.		
The presenter used gestures and body language.		
The presenter spoke clearly and confidently.		
The presenter correctly used words/expressions from the lesson.		

 **Homework**

You are speaking to your co-workers. Write a short ending of a presentation about a company retreat. Then, record yourself giving the presentation. Listen to your recording and think about how you can improve your presentation.

___

Warm Up Sample Answers
1. It's (not / kind of / really) important.
2. My closing are generally (short/long). / It depends on the presentation.
3. (Yes, I / No, I don't) think my closings are usually strong.

Comprehension Check Answers
1. The speaker was talking about the new privacy policy.
2. It is on the whiteboard.

Vocabulary Answers
1. b, 2. c, 3. e, 4. a, 5. d, 6. f

Vocab Test Answers
1. helpful, 2. policy, 3. curious, 4. gain, 5. contact information, 6. Those

Grammar Points Answers
1. a) informative b) enjoyable c) helpful
2. a) working b) meeting c) doing business

Write Sample Answer
I hope the presentation was helpful.
I know many of you wanted to know more about the new service. Perhaps now you have a better understanding.

Real Presentation Sample Answer
I hope the presentation was useful to all of you.
I know many of you were curious about this year's training programs. Perhaps now you have a good idea of what's being offered.
For those wanting more information, just email or call me.
It's been a pleasure talking about the programs.
Again, thank you.

Homework Sample Answer
I hope the presentation was informative.
I know many of you have been curious about the annual company retreat. Perhaps now you have a better understanding of its purpose.
For those wanting more detail, just send me a message.
I want to wrap up by saying it's been a pleasure talking to you about the retreat.
Again, thank you.

Presentation Tip

Closing Your Presentation with Confidence
자신감 있게 프레젠테이션을 마무리하기

You have done a good job with the introduction and the body. Now, you're on the last part of your presentation. It's important to have a strong close. The audience will remember the ending.
도입부와 본론을 잘 진행했다. 이제 마지막 부분에 와 있다. 강한 마무리는 중요하다. 청중은 끝을 기억하기 마련이다.

① Match the tone with the subject. 분위기를 프레젠테이션 주제와 어울리게 유지한다.

Is your presentation about a crisis or risk? Then you should sound serious. Is your presentation trying to persuade the audience? In that case, you should end on a highly enthusiastic note.
위기나 위험에 관한 프레젠테이션인가? 그러면 진지하게 들려야 한다. 청중을 설득하려는 프레젠테이션인가? 그런 경우라면 아주 열광적인 분위기로 마쳐야 한다.

② Restate any decisions made. 결정된 사항을 다시 언급한다.

In some presentations, you need to get a decision from the audience. If a decision was made, restate what that was. If no decision was made, mention this as well.
일부 프레젠테이션에서는 청중으로부터 결정을 받아야 한다. 결정이 내려졌다면 그것이 무엇인지 다시 언급한다. 결정이 이루어지지 않았다면 이 부분도 언급한다.

③ Clarify any action items. 작업 항목을 명확하게 한다.

Are there any actions needed after the presentation? If so, be clear on what they are. Also specify who is responsible for each. Mentioning the due dates is also important.
프레젠테이션이 끝난 후 필요한 작업이 있는가? 그렇다면 그것이 무엇인지 명확하게 한다. 또한 각 작업 항목을 책임질 사람이 누구인지 명시한다. 마감 시한을 언급하는 것도 중요하다.

④ Avoid fizzling out at the end. 흐지부지하게 끝내는 것을 피한다.

If your ending is weak, you reduce the impact of your entire presentation. Don't end with, "Okay, that's all." Remain focused and upbeat. You might say with confidence, "Again, thank you!"
마무리가 약하면, 전체 프레젠테이션의 임팩트를 떨어뜨린다. '자, 끝났습니다'로 끝내지 말자. 집중력과 긍정적인 분위기를 유지하자. 자신있게 '다시 한번 감사드립니다!'라고 할 수 있다.

12 Answering Questions

 Learning Objectives

- Learners can answer audience questions.
- Learners can commend an audience member for asking a good question.
- Learners can address any further concerns the audience might have.

 Warm Up

Work with a partner or in a group. Discuss the following questions.

1. Why should a presentation include a Q&A session?
2. In your own presentations, how long does a Q&A generally take?
3. Do you often get difficult questions during Q&A?

Sample Presentation Script

Read the presentation aloud.

That's a great question, and I'm glad you asked that. What you're asking is if we have the tools necessary to take on the project.

The answer is definitely "yes." We have the staff and the infrastructure.

Now, you might be concerned about our lack of experience in handling big tasks like this one.

Allow me to clarify a few things.

그건 아주 좋은 질문이고, 물어보셔서 감사합니다. 저희가 프로젝트를 수행하는 데 필요한 도구가 있는지 물어보셨군요.

답변은 확실히 '네'입니다. 저희는 직원과 인프라가 있습니다.

자, 저희에게 이런 큰 작업을 맡기는 데 경험이 부족한 것에 대해 걱정하실 수 있습니다.

몇 가지를 명확하게 설명해 드리겠습니다.

✓ Comprehension Check

Answer the questions.

1. What does the speaker say the answer is?
2. What lack of experience is the speaker talking about?

 **Vocabulary**

Match the words or expressions with the correct definitions.

1. tool _____	a. 필요한
2. necessary _____	b. ~에 대해 걱정하다
3. infrastructure _____	c. 도구
4. be concerned about _____	d. 명확하게 설명하다
5. lack of _____	e. ~의 부족
6. clarify _____	f. 인프라

✓ Vocab Test

Fill in the blanks with the correct words or expressions.

tools / necessary / infrastructure / am concerned about / lack of / clarify

1. Is that really _____?
2. I _____ the delays.
3. You need to use the right _____.
4. Could you _____ something?
5. The problem is the _____ resources.
6. We do have many _____ projects.

⊕ Bonus Resources

the million-dollar question 매우 중요한 질문

A: Do you think Mason will accept our price? Mason이 우리 가격을 수락할까요?
B: That is **the million-dollar question**. 그것이 아주 중요한 질문이죠.

영국과 미국의 〈Who Wants to be a Millionaire?(누가 백만장자가 되고 싶은가?)〉라는 TV 프로그램에서 유래됐다고 한다. 프로그램의 마지막 질문이 바로 매우 답변하기 어려운, 백만 달러를 주는 the million-dollar question이기 때문이다.

Grammar Points

Read the following and practice making sentences.

1. That's a great question, and I ~

> That's a great question은 '그건 아주 좋은 질문입니다'를, and I ~ 는 '그리고 저는 ~'을 의미한다. 우선 상대방의 질문에 대해 칭찬을 한 후 그에 대응하는 무언가를 언급하는 표현이다.
>
> 📖 *That's a great question, and I can answer that.*
>   그건 아주 좋은 질문이고, 그것에 대해서 대답할 수 있습니다.

a) That's a great question, and I _____ that a little later.
   그건 아주 좋은 질문이고, 조금 있다가 답변을 드리겠습니다.

b) That's a great question, and I _____ Dennis to answer that.
   그건 아주 좋은 질문이고, Dennis가 답변해 주셨으면 합니다.

c) That's a great question, and I _____ you asked that.
   그건 아주 좋은 질문이고, 왜 그것을 물어보셨는지 압니다.

2. Allow me to ~

> Allow me to ~에서 allow는 '내가 ~을 하게 허락해 달라'가 아니라 실은 '내가 ~하겠습니다'를 말한다는 뜻이다. 비교적 격식을 차린 표현이라고 할 수 있다.
>
> 📖 *Allow me to explain.* 설명해 드리겠습니다.

a) Allow me to _____ you an example. 하나의 예를 들어보겠습니다.

b) Allow me to _____ a suggestion. 제안을 하나 드리겠습니다.

c) Allow me to _____ on that. 그것에 대해 자세히 설명해 드리겠습니다.

 **Practice**

Making Sentences

Practice writing sentences. Use the given words or use your own. Then, read your sentences to your partner or group.

1. What you're asking is ~
   (if we know / why that is / whether that's true)

   - _____
   - _____
   - _____

2. You might be concerned about ~
   (the delay / our schedule / these issues)

   - _____
   - _____
   - _____

Write

Write a short presentation script that briefly acknowledges a question and gives a short answer.

_____
_____
_____

Real Presentation

Read the scenario and the four key items on the flashcard. Then, answer the audience's questions. When another member of your group presents, use the checklist below.

Scenario

> You are a sales manager for a manufacturing company. You've just finished presenting to some new customers about a large order of laptops. You're now in the middle of answering a question. They are asking if you can get the laptops delivered by November. Say "yes" and tell them that you already have the laptops in stock. Also assure them that there won't be any shipping delays.

Flashcard

1. deliver the laptops by November? Yes.	2. already in stock
3. concerned about possible shipping delays	4. no delays

✓ Presentation Checklist	Y	N
The presenter made eye contact with the audience.		
The presenter used gestures and body language.		
The presenter spoke clearly and confidently.		
The presenter correctly used words/expressions from the lesson.		

 **Homework**

You are speaking to some executives of a company that might become a partner. Write a short answer to a question about a potential partnership. Then, record yourself giving the presentation. Listen to your recording and think about how you can improve your presentation.

_____
_____
_____

Warm Up Sample Answers
1. Because it (allows the audience to ask questions / makes the presentation more interactive / can show that the presenter is knowledgeable).
2. It generally takes (a few minutes / less than 10 minutes / about 30 minutes).
3. (Yes, I / No, I don't) often get difficult questions.

Comprehension Check Answers
1. The speakers says the answer is "yes."
2. The speaker is talking about their lack of experience in handling big tasks.

Vocabulary Answers
1. c, 2. a, 3. f, 4. b, 5. e, 6. d

Vocab Test Answers
1. necessary, 2. am concerned about, 3. tools, 4. clarify, 5. lack of, 6. infrastructure

Grammar Points Answers
1. a) will answer b) would like c) know why
2. a) give b) make/offer c) elaborate

Write Sample Answer
That's a great question, and I'm happy to answer that. What you're asking is if we will be launching a new product this year. The answer is "yes." We will be launching a spicy flavor of our potato chips.

Real Presentation Sample Answer
That's a great question, and I can answer that easily. What you're asking is if we can deliver the laptops by November. The answer is "yes." We already have them in stock.
You might be concerned about possible shipping delays.
Allow me to assure you that there won't be any delays.

Homework Sample Answer
That's a great question, and I was waiting for that. In fact, that is the million-dollar question. What you're asking is if we are willing to go into a partnership with you.
The answer is "yes!"
Now, you might be concerned about our government's regulations.
Allow me to briefly tell you about them.

Presentation Tip

How to Handle Questions Effectively
질문을 잘 다루는 방법

Q&A time can be the most important part of your presentation. Prepare beforehand. Also, maintain your composure during the presentation.
Q&A 시간이 프레젠테이션의 가장 중요한 순간이 될 수 있다. 미리 준비하자. 또한, 프레젠테이션 중에는 평정을 유지한다.

① Prepare in advance. 사전에 준비한다.

Think about who will be attending. Then consider what their concerns might be. That way, you can anticipate possible questions. Come up with some answers.

누가 참석할 것인지 생각해 본다. 그런 후 그들의 우려가 무엇일지 고려한다. 그러면 어떤 질문이 나올지 예상해 볼 수 있다. 답변을 준비한다.

② Establish guidelines. 가이드라인을 정한다.

Let the audience know the time allotted for Q&A. You might also tell them how many questions each person can ask. Of course, in many cases, you can't control the Q&A. For example, your audience might consist of upper management or clients.

Q&A에 할당된 시간을 청중에게 알린다. 한 사람당 몇 개의 질문을 할 수 있는지 알려줄 수도 있다. 물론 많은 경우에는 Q&A를 제어할 수 없다. 예를 들어 청중이 고위 관리층이나 고객일 수 있기 때문이다.

③ Confirm the question. 질문을 확인한다.

In general, it's good to repeat the question. You can confirm your understanding. You can also make sure the audience heard the question.

일반적으로 질문을 다시 말하는 것이 좋다. 내가 이해했는지 확인할 수 있다. 또한 청중이 질문을 잘 들었는지 확인할 수 있다.

④ Don't evade a question. 질문을 회피하지 않는다.

You might be asked a difficult question. Don't try to evade it. If you don't have an answer, offer to get back to the person later. Sometimes the question isn't relevant. If so, say you'll meet with the person after the presentation to discuss it further.

어려운 질문을 받을 수도 있다. 회피하지 말자. 대답할 수 없다면 나중에 그 사람에게 연락한다고 한다. 때로는 질문이 주제와 관련이 없을 수 있다. 이럴 때는 프레젠테이션이 끝나고 따로 설명해 준다고 말하자.

MEMO